W. Knox Wigram

Twelve wonderful Tales told in Rhyme

W. Knox Wigram

Twelve wonderful Tales told in Rhyme

ISBN/EAN: 9783337120610

Printed in Europe, USA, Canada, Australia, Japan

Cover: Foto ©ninafisch / pixelio.de

More available books at **www.hansebooks.com**

TWELVE WONDERFUL TALES

TOLD IN RHYME

BY

W. KNOX WIGRAM,

AUTHOR OF "FIVE HUNDRED POUNDS REWARD."

WITH ILLUSTRATIONS BY JOHN L. ROGET.

LONDON:
RICHARD BENTLEY, NEW BURLINGTON STREET,
Publisher in Ordinary to Her Majesty.
1870.

LONDON
R. CLAY, SONS, AND TAYLOR, PRINTERS,
BREAD STREET HILL.

Contents.

TWELVE WONDERFUL TALES,

TO WIT.

		PAGE
I.	THE LITTLE HUNCHBACK	1
II.	THE JAR OF GOLD	21
III.	THE FLYING HORSE	30
IV.	CAPTAIN TINDERBOX	67
V.	EMMA AND EGINARD	81
VI.	THE CONJUROR'S CALL	98
VII.	THE ROSE OF BASSORA	105
VIII.	ERMENGARDE	112
IX.	PETER AND TULIP	129
X.	DOOM OF THE BRIEFLESS	142
XI.	POETRY *versus* SCIENCE	159
XII.	ORIANDE	173

PREFACE.

To deliver myself at once from the charge of trucking off 'Old Lamps for New,' I hereby, in Market Overt, declare that several of the pieces following were comprised in a certain volume entitled 'Flotsam and Jetsam; a Cargo of Christmas Rhyme,' published a certain number of years ago.

That book has long since been out of print. And the good-natured proposal of my friend Mr. Roget, to use his etching-needle in my service, in case I liked to take another rub at these Old Lamps, has resulted in the present Apparition.

Much of what follows has more recently seen the light, in the pages of TEMPLE BAR.

I have also exhumed from its rest (in Bentley's Miscellany) a vagary entitled 'Poetry *versus* Science,' evolved whilst I was a freshman at Trinity; the rabid undergraduatism of which it would be idle to attempt to mitigate by any maturer touch.

I have preserved an invocation addressed to the late Lord Macaulay, in another extract from the said Miscellany, printed whilst he was yet in the zenith of his living fame.

LONDON,
Dec. 1, 1869.

TWELVE WONDERFUL TALES,

ETC.

THE LITTLE HUNCHBACK.

A LEAF FROM THE ARABIAN NIGHTS.

> 'Publica materies privati juris erit, si
> Nec circa vilem patulumque moraberis orbem;
> Nec verbum verbo curabis reddere fidus
> Interpres.'

CASGAR! Turbans everywhere. Turbans I say.
Upstairs and downstairs and over the way.
Turbans of every conceivable hue,
Scarlet and orange and indigo-blue.
Come, don't contradict me! Because if you do,
I'll multiply every Turk's turban by two.

In a certain snug street that I know very well,—
For I lived in Casgar once, a year at a spell,
And dashed off one morning, myself, in a hurry,
The 'plan of the city' that's published in 'Murray'—
There lives, or did live, a most popular party;
A tailor called Mustapha, civil and hearty.

So merry withal,
You never could call
But you'd hear him strike up like the band at a ball!
Such fun was his music that people would stop
And form quite a crowd round the door of the shop;
Till many a Turk, irresistibly pleasured,
Who stayed there to listen, stepped in to be measured.

One fine afternoon,
Towards the middle of June,
Our friend was as usual humming a tune
And singing some verses he'd made on the moon,
As cross-legged he cosily squatted at work,
In his double capacity, Tailor and Turk;
When a queer little figure
As black as a nigger
Peeped in at the door with a wink and a snigger;
On his backbone a hunch
Had grown such a bunch
That he looked very much like an African Punch,
And Mustapha's heart gave a leap to his throat
Lest what he might want was a ready-made coat.

But it wasn't: he sat
Plump down on the mat,
And drummed a few chords on the crown of his hat,
Then struck up a ballad so brimful of fun
That Snip rolled about on his board like a tun,
Shouting, 'Stop there, you grinning young son of a gun!
Don't burst a man's biler, adone lad, adone!'

But stop?—not a bit! he rattled his wit
Till Mustapha's ribs were just ready to split,
It's a mercy he didn't go off in a fit!

The words I can't copy—because, in a ramble,
My pockets were picked by a bandit of Stamboul,
Who prigged all my papers and pounded my head—
Walked off in my breeches, and left me for dead.
I only remember it closed with a wink,
And a pointed request for 'a trifle to drink.'

   ' Drink ?—dear little black,
    With a hump on your back,'
Cried Mustapha, ' come along home for a snack !
    The cut of your jib
    Will tickle my 'rib,'
We'll stand you a supper and liquor *ad lib.*
Right well you deserve it. Come, jump off the floor,
And shove up the shutters whilst I lock the door.
Early Closing for ever, and Mental Improvement !
I say, little dog, it's an excellent movement.'

   Not far down the road
    Lay the Tailor's abode,
His ' cot ' as he termed it when turning an ode,
Where the fondest of wives, with a kiss on her lips,
Stood ready to welcome the fondest of Snips.

   With a start and a stare,
    The Tailoress fair
Exclaimed, ' Oh my goodness, who have you got there ?
A little black Blackamoor ? Well, I declare !
' Pray, wife,' said the Tailor, 'some supper prepare :
Don't snub little Hunchback, but set him a chair ;
If he doesn't surprise you, when once his tongue's loose,
By the bones of the Prophet, I'll swallow my goose!'

   Alas and alack
    For our dear little Black,

His manners were almost as queer as his back :
For he never said 'thank you,' and never said 'please,'
But ate with his knife, and began with his cheese;
    And snored as he chewed,
    Which is awfully rude,
When in civilized company taking your food :
Till his host and his hostess exclaimed, 'What a glutton
This low little Hunchback is, over his mutton !'

    At length a great crab
    He snatched with a grab,
And down his black throttle attempted to dab;
    But frightful to say,
    It 'went the wrong way,'
And there, its crustaceous ill-will to display,
    Perversely stuck fast.
    'I'm diddled at last !'
Gasped Blacky. 'Gulp—guggle. It . . cannot . . get . . past.
Hi !—Slap my back somebody—Oh, try a spoon !
A long one—a longer ! Oh, I'm a gone 'coon !'

    To paint the despair
    Of our kind-hearted pair,
When poor little Hunchback rolled out of his chair,
I give you my honour is more than I dare :
For thus it is writ in the Laws of Casgar :—
(I practised myself many months at the bar
Of their principal Court—called the 'Judgment Bazaar,'
And therefore can safely state facts as they are,)
'𝔍𝔣 𝔞𝔫𝔶 𝔱𝔯𝔲𝔢 𝔐𝔲𝔰𝔰𝔲𝔩𝔪𝔞𝔫 𝔡𝔦𝔢𝔰 𝔦𝔫 𝔶𝔬𝔲𝔯 𝔥𝔬𝔲𝔰𝔢,
𝔜𝔬𝔲'𝔩𝔩 𝔟𝔢 𝔥𝔲𝔫𝔤 𝔱𝔥𝔢 𝔫𝔢𝔵𝔱 𝔡𝔞𝔶'—which seems rather a chouse.
So it's clear that our couple had reasons a few
For bringing their crooked young visitor to.

They ran off directly for 'Hints on Emergencies,'
To see what the author (an eminent surgeon) says;
   They opened his jaw,
   And fished in his maw
With hook-sticks and scissors, and stammered 'Oh law!'
When they couldn't so much as catch hold of a claw.
   'It's all of no use,'
   Said the Tailor, 'the deuce
Take the hunch and the boy! they'll be cooking my goose,
I expect, with a stock that ain't easy to loose,
   To-morrow at six;
   It's rather a fix,
At my time of life to be in for the kicks!
Come, what's to be done wife, eh?—chop him up little,
And sell him for sav'loys and poor people's victual?
Or, stay! Lug him off to our neighbour the Saw-bones,
And swear that *he* killed him, in opening his jaw-bones!
That's better! yes, bundle him up on my back:
I'll leave him next door and be home in a crack!'

   'Ding ding' at the bell:
   'This gemman ain't well,'
Says the Tailor, 'his backbone's beginnin' to swell.
Tell your master, my lad: say he's bustin' with pain,
And sends up this guinea his case to explain:
And tell him he'd better come down pretty quick,
Or he'll find his poor patient as dead as a brick.
And stay,—since your passage is preciously cold—
Let's run him upstairs to the landing:—lay hold!'

   Our doctor—a Jew,
   Had but little to do,
Because all his patients were luckily few;
So he sat in his room, looking hungry and blue,

Writing fancy prescriptions and fabulous letters,
And wishing himself better known to his betters.
   And, of course, when his boy
   Burst in, full of joy,
' O, master—O, master—O, master, ahoy!
   Here's a cove and a pound!
   And, O, isn't he round!
And the little chap squeaks as he sits on the ground!
And he can't walk about, 'cause he's bad I'll be bound!'
   He bounced off his chair,
   Six feet in the air,
And taking, alas, neither candle nor care,
Went hop skip and jump to the top of the stair—
   Where, just in the way,
   Poor Blackamoor lay,
By no means expecting such nimble display—
Kicked him head over heels—O, it's painful to say
   How he banged like a ball
   On the stairs and the wall,
And how bump after bump you might hear in his fall,
Till at last you might hear him roll into the hall.

   ' O! O! Vat ish here?
   I've killed him, I fear!
Pray fetch down the candlesh! O Mosesh, ma tear,
Pleash help us—I vould not have kicked on his rear
   If I'd known vere he lay.
   O! vat a bad day,
To valk on von's patient that comes vith his pay!'
So shrieked the physician as down stairs he ran
In frantic pursuit of the poor little man:
   He did all he could,
   But he did no more good
Than if he'd been coaxing a doll made of wood;

> For every appliance
> Of surgical science
> He found that his customer held at defiance,
> And still perseveringly lay on the floor,
> Precisely as ugly and dead as before.
> Then loudly and long did the doctor give tongue,
> Crying, 'Look vat a pity it is to be hung!'

It was well for this Jew that his little foot-page,
Though small, was extremely discreet for his age.
He never with lollipop made himself ill,
Nor cribbed from the counter, nor stole from the till,
Nor whistled on Sunday, but sat by the cook,
Improving her mind with some good little book:
And he often would say—'See, I never get whacked,
And I never say nothing that isn't a fact,
And in minding my work, O I'm always exact,
And perhaps, when I die, I'll be put in a Tract;
That's 'cause I'm so good, cook: indeed I don't see
As the "Little Blind Dustman" was better than me.'

'Oh master, oh master!' the prodigy said,
'O don't go a-twistin' the hair off your head,
If so be as the poor little gemman is dead!
And please not to swear—'cause I'll quote you a text——'

> 'Texsh be blowed,' said the Jew, 'you young beggar, what next?
> I've killed him, I tellsh you!—He's dead as de door,
> And if de polishemen shall find him, oh lor!
> De Judgsh and John Ketch vill be only two stages——'

'Boo-hoo!' cried the youth, 'shall I lose my week's wages?
  Oh master, hooray!
  I've thought of a way;

You needn't be hung, for I'm sure it will pay—
And I'll tell you for sixpence ! come, what do you say?
Step out on the roof and, O my, what a lark !
Through the chimney next door shove him down in the
    dark !
If you swear that he never came into the house,
Though I can't tell a lie, I'll be mute as a mouse ;
And then, in your stead, up the ladder will go, sir,
Our neighbour, the Wholesale and Family Grocer !'

' Oh Mosesh !' the Jew said, 'dis queer leetle brute,
Dear boy, down the chimnesh we surely will shoot ;
And, for fear in de vay he should shmut all his clothes,
Ve'd mush better keep dem ourshelves, I suppose.
I'll pull off his coat vich, ma tear, is quite new,
And a great deal too goot for to vear in a flue ;
You pick off de breeshes and shoes from his fork,
He von't vant again to go out for a valk !'
So the poor little Black, being stripped on the spot,
Down the chimney of Cofi, the grocer, was shot.

Now Cofi, the grocer, though upright as any,
Except in the matter of turning a penny,
Was given to practise, I'm sadly afraid,
What are mildly described as ' the tricks of the trade.'
      At least, people said,
      With a shake of the head,
That he primed his ' prime congo ' with sloes and black-
    lead :
And, worse a great deal, that, unpleasantly often,
With him ' ripe old coffee ' meant ' rotten old coffin ; '
A dodge which they tell me, to this very day,
Is practised in London—don't mention it, pray—

And that people quite like, if they'd only but speak up,
A dash of their grandmamma whisked in the teacup.[1]
His sugar, they added, was sandy and damp,
And his oil only fit for a 'wonderful lamp;'
In fact, all agreed, if he wasn't a scamp,
The Grocer was certainly one of that stamp.
Of course on such gossip I'd gladly be dumb,
But it bears on my story—so out it must come.

For there lived in the city a well-meaning man,
  Who'd found out a plan
  Such rogues to trepan,
And rolls from the oven and milk from the can
  Would buy on the sly,
  On purpose to try,
As he sat at his breakfast with nobody by,
And a shining brass microscope screwed in his eye,
  If the bread was quite nice,
  And hadn't a spice
Of something that wouldn't be cheap at the price,
And the milk just the thing that the real cow carries,
Unmixed with pump-water and plaster of Paris:
Until, when he'd quite made the tour of the table,
He'd slash off an article, caustic and able,
  In a work of his own,
  Where all would be shown,
And horrified spinsters would read it and groan,
'Oh why don't he let people's victuals alone?'

---

[1] The researches of the 'Analytical Sanitary Commission,' conducted by the Editor of *The Lancet*, were in full swing when these lines were written. Among the many unlawful ingredients detected or suspected in prime old Mocha, as retailed at various advertising establishments, an awful *haut goût* in the way of elm-sawdust from decayed coffin-wood was certainly talked about.

Oh why did he tell us ? No wonder one's thin !
Oh dear, what a state must our stomachs be in !'

   After this you may guess
   That Cofi no less
Went walking in bodily fear of 'the press,'
Than of some one whose name I discreetly suppress ;
And passed all his time in an exquisite funk,
Or only felt passably valiant when drunk.

That evening, however, he'd been to a ball,
And came singing home, by the help of the wall,
Declaring he scarcely felt frightened at all.
   He entered his shop
   With a rollicking hop,
That proved, pretty plainly, he'd 'just had a drop,'
   And, waving his glim,
   Cried, 'Let me catch *him*—
Old Spoil-sport ! I'll mangle him, body and limb !
   Who says I'm afeard ?
   If old Bogey appeared,
This minute, I'd take him, like this, by the beard,
Give him one for his tail, sir, and two for his nob,—
Great Allah defend us ! *Who's that on the hob ?*
   O look at it—look !
   It's back's all a-crook !
If a baby gorilla'd been boiled by the cook,
It couldn't look worse ! O I see—I mistook !
I know him ! The dirty Informer, stark naked !
Here's a chance at his noddle !—by jingo, I'll take it !'
Whack—bang, ' Take another ! You came for a sample ?
Oh, did you ?' bang—whack—'you shall have it and ample.'
Crack—bang, 'Do you like it ? Oh dear, it's no trouble,
Not even,' bang—crack, 'if I gave it you double !

Come bolt, sir, and own
The forbearance I've shown!
You won't! O, I'll make you! Don't think you'll atone
For . . . O, my good gracious, he's cold as a stone!
Oh Cofi! why couldn't you let him alone?
Ah, wretch that I am, may I ne'er smoke tobacco more
If I ain't been and done it—I've murdered the Blackamoor!'

. In a moment he saw
The fiends of the Law
Popping up from till, canister, counter, and drawer,
Scowling, howling, and growling, with halter in claw!
The candle burnt blue
And the gibbering crew
Screamed, 'Cofi—come Cofi, we're waiting for you!
Don't keep us all night!'
In short such a sight
As 'powerful writers,' who doubtless are right,
Persist in purveying for circles polite,
Whenever for murder they chance to indict;
All which made the matter prodigiously black,
And took the poor Grocer completely aback.
And, sobered of course,
He roared with remorse,
So loud that it almost attracted 'the force,'
Whose sympathy's rather a doubtful resource;—
Since—even in Bow-street—those gemmen in blue
Are apt to think less of your victim than *you*.

He snatched up the body—ran out in the street—
(A 50 was, luckily, munching cold meat
Adown the Jew's 'airey,' that lay on his beat,
And trying *his* hand at improving the cook,
Though not, I'm afraid, with a 'good little book')—

Stuck him fast by the wall,
Ran back with a squall,
And jumped into bed, breeches, turban, and all;
Where, all the long night through, he lay on the rack,
And squealed through the sheets like a pig in a sack.

That night, it so happened, the 'Friends of the Vicious,'
A clique in Casgar then extremely officious,
Had held High Palaver in 'Brotherhood Hall,'
To prove that the heathen weren't vicious at all:
That all men were brothers, and all men should hug,
Or as they expressed it, 'drink out of one mug;'
     Going on to proclaim
     That, if 'twas your aim
To make shaggy savages humble and tame,
'Twasn't powder and ball would accomplish that same.
    'You should first catch a Tartar,
    And coax him to barter,'
Said they, 'and the moment he finds what you're after,
    He'll say with a grin,
    Extending his fin,
" My dear Preachee-Teachee, now don't take me in!
I'm backward at figures, you'll find, I'm afraid,
But I and my nation will joyfully trade."'

'It merely,' they said, 'wanted skilful caressing
To make the poor Bushman a positive blessing:
We should bear with his freaks:—if he did in the night
Drive your cattle and leave half your haystacks alight,
Should you for that reason—yes, you—better taught,
Humanity's precepts hold likewise at naught?
Not so! Talk of friendship and fifty per cent.—
Then dance and rub noses all round in a tent!

You'll send him clocks, calico, tweezers, and rum,
In 'change for scalps, elephants, banjos, and gum;
Won't *that* be a triumph—a glory withal,
To the nation that boasts of a Brotherhood Hall!'

'Twas thus, from the platform, with unction and zest,
Sneeki-Peeki, the Quaker, that conclave addressed.
'Twas thrilling, they tell me, to hear him, as ' cheers'—
Condensed in ' sensation'—subsided in ' tears ;'
And heavy old women and hazy old cits,
Were heard through the darkness, exploding in fits.
At length, having fairly disburdened his mind,
Proved that battles were sinful and blows were unkind,
Sneeki-Peeki, the Quaker, first pouching his fee—
Went smiling benignantly home to his tea.

   I wonder why Fate
   Lies always in wait,
Such excellent people to catch in a strait,
And why I've this dismal mishap to relate ?
In crossing the Grocer's respectable street,
Where little dead Hunchback stood stiff on his feet,
   Just outside the shop,
   The Quaker ran flop,
Against the poor body, which caused it to drop,
Tripping up Sneeki-Peeki, who gave a great hop,
Crying, 'Thieves ! here, policemen !—hoy, watchmen—
 patrol !
I'm robbed—I'm assaulted ! I am, 'pon my soul !
Come, somebody, come ! I'm in fear of my life !
Come, some one, before he jumps up with a knife !'

   But then, when he found
   His foe on the ground
Didn't look very large, and was crooked and round,

　　　　He bravely ran back
　　　　And hit him a whack,
Shouting 'Shamming's no use, you detestable Black!
I'll teach you a peaceable man to attack!
Oh, you don't mean to rise! you're afraid of my stick?
Very well, then you're all the more handy to kick!
Ha, here come the Watch! they shall hear what you've
　　done!'
Cried the Watch—'Hollo, Quaker, it's useless to run!
No nonsense! we saw you—we watched the whole tussle,
　　man;
And saw you knock over and pound this 'ere Mussulman.
If he's dead—and he is too! we wouldn't be you,
When the first thing to-morrow, you're catching your due!'

　　　　Of course it was vain
　　　　The facts to explain,
Such flimsy evasions, where autocrats reign,
Deservedly meeting with simple disdain:
And poor Sneeki-Peeki, with great consternation,
In five minutes found himself tight in the Station.

It seems in Casgar, where but slenderly thrives
The noble Profession that somehow contrives
To run rather to seed in our Westminster hives,
The County-Court Judges try folks for their lives;
And it's found that this practice, in dealing with crime,
Effects both a saving of money and time.

　　　　They 'call on' the cause,
　　　　And nobody jaws
About 'precedents,' 'proofs,' and absurd little 'flaws,'
Which would argue a great disrespect for the laws.

'Now then,' roars the Judge, 'where's the Quaker? who—
    that?
That sheep-stealing, snuff-coloured hound in a hat?
Knock it off, sirrah Tipstaff! now then—what's the charge?
"Broke a Mussulman's head and the Statutes at large?"
Of course he did! Look at him—guilty and dumb—
Not an answer to make!—Tell the hangman to come!
Hold your tongue, sir, this moment! D'ye think I sit here
To hear fellows chatter whose guilt is quite clear?',

'Jack Ketch, my Lord, waits.'
                'Oh, that's lucky; away!
Tie him up—tie him up, lying rascal! and stay,—
Set a chair for the Court, outside, under a tree,
That the end of this villain myself I may see.'

Loud roared Sneeki-Peeki, on finding his case
Assume such a sudden and shocking bad face;
(Any practical man could have told him 'twas vain
His private antipathies thus to explain.)
        The rope was made fast,
        The moment was past,
Which florid reporters describe as one's 'last;'
When somebody shouted, 'Stop, hangman! avast!
        You've got the wrong cove;
        Don't let him be hove!
He isn't the villain—I did it, by Jove!
I'm Cofi—the Grocer! I caught him last night
Making mouths on my hob, and I smashed him outright,
And I can't go to sleep 'cause I'm jumping with fright,
And I wish to be hanged, and oh! please tie me tight!'

'Lor' bless me,' the Judge said, 'if this be the case,
You'd better step up in the gentleman's place.

I'll be bound, if the facts are at all as you say,
That thief, Sneeki-Peeki, won't stand in your way!'

So up went the Grocer :—his head's through the noose,
In a precious fair way to be cured of the blues ;
      When hark, there's a cry,
        'Dear Judgsh, it vash I,
And I cannot permit de pore Grosher to die !
Don't hang him, I ask, and I vish to tell vy !'

' Good heavens,' the Judge said, ' suppose it *were* you !
Why keep the Court waiting, you snivelling Jew?
Jump up and be hanged without further to-do !'

' But I vish to speak vords—may I ?—only a few ? '

' NO, YOU MAYN'T !' roared the Judge, ' for they wouldn't
    be true !
Pitch over the Grocer there, hangman, and stifle
The beggar who'd thus with our dignity trifle.'

' Ay, ay, sir,' the hangman said, ' how many more ?
Here's three to begin with—and here's number four !
My stars, merry Mustapha ! well, I *am* blessed !
If he isn't as great a tom-fool as the rest !'

' My lord,' cried the Tailor, ' one word in your ear !'
But, just as he spoke, people shouted, ' Stand clear !
Make way there—make way for our Lord the Vizier !'

' Bang, bang !' go the kettle-drums, twelve on a side,
That roll for his Greatness where'er he may ride ;
Flap, flap, go the standards of Mussulman green,
That flutter wherever his Greatness is seen ;

'Hooray!' go the people, who always hooray
At aught that's unwontedly noisy or gay;
And down goes the Court in a servile salaam,
As much as to say, 'Oh, how flattered I am!
I hope you don't mean to play Wolf to my Lamb!'

   'Rise, Judge, to your feet;
    Your worship I greet
From one who esteems you both just and discreet.
The Lord of the Faithful, who sits all alone,
And rules the wide world upon Solomon's throne,
Commands your attendance; and bids me require
Both Tailor, and Doctor, and Grocer, and Liar:
It seeming that one of them's murdered his Laureate,
A dark and disloyal performance to glory at:—
He hears they all own it, and swears by the moon
He'll teach them to bully a Royal Buffoon!'

   Now, just at this point,
    My tale to disjoint,
I bid all at once lesser actors 'aroint!'—
Now for a goose-quill, round and clean,—
Now for our crowning change of scene!

   That morning at eight,
    From his pillow of state
And couch of spun-gold, Caliph Haroun the Great
Woke, yawning extremely and scratching his pate.
'Go, some one,' said he, 'for our funny Buffoon,
And bid him come hither and strike up a tune:
We're seedy this morning,—yes, rather so-so:
Our Hunchback alone can inspirit us.—Go!'

' Great Prince of the Earth, and the Air, and the Wave,
Live long and for ever!' made answer the slave.
' His Royal Buffoonship, Sir, yesterday night,
Alas, closed his eyes on your majesty's light:
He went for a walk, and O, shocking to tell,
Strolled into some place where the tradespeople dwell;
They caught him—they killed him, and, stranger than all,
They're crowding like fun to the County Court Hall,
Each swearing, "I did it! 'tis I that should squeak,"
Which looks like a dodge, Sir, to puzzle the beak.'

Upstarted in wrath from his pillow of state
And couch of spun-gold Caliph Haroun the Great;
  For dearer than all
  In the Caliphat Hall
Was the blithe little Hunchback so funny and small.
' Is it thus,' he exclaimed, ' that these worms of the dust
Presume to insult Caliph Haroun the Just?
Must he mourn the pet boy that delighted him so,
And the girls of his Harem their little black beau,
And mourn unrevenged? no, by Mahomet, no!
  Command our Vizier
  To bring every one here,
Before our tribunal at once to appear;
For, by Heaven, the ears of all ages shall ring
With the sentence they'll hear from the lips of their King!'

  'Tis done, as we know:
  And, bowing quite low,
They front the stern judgment-seat all in a row,
Sneeki-Peeki included—the picture of woe,
With his eloquent mouth like a capital O.

' Curst wretches!' the Caliph said, ' which of ye four
Slew this poor little fellow that lies on the floor,

The pet of our Palace, the joy of our wives?
Beware how ye answer : ye plead for your lives.'

Then the Tailor spoke first, and the Jew, in his turn,
Gave the tale to the Grocer, and then, ' wretched kern,'
The Quaker, who sorely mistrusted such parley,
Contrived, with loud sobs, to blurt out the *finale*.

   When all had been heard,
    ' It's rather absurd ! '
Said the Caliph. 'We think the first, second, and third
May pass without censure :—the crab and the kick
Were accidents purely, and, as for the stick,
Master Grocer, next time, you must mind who you lick.
But, as for the last,' he resumed with a smile,
' Sneeki-Peeki, your head must come out of its tile ;
For, of course, when we look on this poor little dumb body,
We want consolation for this out of somebody !
Ho, headsman ! '
   The words were scarce uttered when, lo !
With a queer little kick and a queer little crow,
   The queer little man
    Sat up, and began
To sneeze and crack jokes and his visage to fan,
Saying, ' Fetch me some beer, please, as soon as you can !
I'm faint and I'm dry as the dust in the pan ;
Do, there's a good Caliph ! now don't look so cross !
I know that, last night, I took too much—fish sauce ! '.

To paint the good Caliph's excessive delight
Would fill a great volume, too bulky to write ;
He let off the steam in a waltz round the garden
And wound up the *pas* with a general pardon.

And then—to conclude—that their fortunate lot,
Like Gunpowder Treason, might ne'er be forgot,
And that all men, for ever and ever, might learn
How difficult sometimes is Truth to discern—
That all one can see of a case may be small,
And black may be white, if one did but know all,
He sent out and bought a great Pillar of Brass,
To stand by the gate where the magistrates pass;
   And bade, on its face,
   From the crown to the base,
A famous Historian write the whole case:
   Which he did, with great skill,
   And it's legible still,
And I own I shall take it prodigiously ill,
If, treating a poet's assertion as *nil*,
You whip your red 'Murray' down out of the shelf,
And rudely demand if I've seen it myself?

THE JAR OF GOLD.

'In England, as among the feudists, the punishment of such as concealed from the King the finding of hidden treasure was formerly no less than death; but *now* it is only fine and imprisonment.'—
BLACKSTONE, A.D. 1765.

STAND forward, you sturdy old peasant,
   And coax the good wife to walk in;
Make bows to the company present,
   And call yourselves Jerry and Jinn.

There!—started at once, what an ocean
   Of circumlocution we sink!
I don't want to boast of the notion—
   I seldom say all that I think.

They lived in a clean little hovel,
   That stood in a garden of greens;
And Jerry dug hard with a shovel,
   While Jinn made the most of their means.

No infants had come to impauper—
   And this was decidedly wrong—
But darning, and cooking, and copper,
   Kept Jinn busy all the day long.

'It's lucky, in fact, that we're able
  To live,' Jerry said, 'as we do.
I always end "Grace before Table"
  With—Law, how six children would chew!'

And so they dwelt, almost contented,
  Though Jerry prayed hard for a sow;
While Jinn, just as frequently, vented
  Her wish for an Alderney cow.

One day—that redoubtable epoch,
  When always *che sara sará*—
In clearing a drain with his reap-hook,
  Says Jerry, 'What's this? Why, a Jar!

'A Jar, as I live! and too heavy,
  Almost, for a person to pull.
I wish that our double-strong nephy
  Was here, with his back like a bull.

'Ah! times were when Jerry could tackle
  A matter o' four times the weight
That now makes his marrow-bones crackle,
  Like so many sticks in a grate.

  * * * * *

'Ho, Jinn, drop your dishclout and kettle!
  Ho, jump, Jinn, and open your eyes!
A Jar, Jinn—all soldered with metal!
  I'd not take a pound for the prize.

'What *can* it be full of, I wonder?'
  'No call to go guessing,' Jinn cried.
'The sooner we crack it asunder,
  The sooner we'll see the inside.'

'Bang, bang!' how they beat and they battered!
   At last a great stopper flew out;
And the kitchen was sprinkled and scattered
   With gold that ran rolling about!

'Whew!' whistled at once Jinn and Jerry;
   'Was ever such wonder-luck known?
Who ever went this for to bury,
   And leave it us all for our own?

'Came ever good fortune so sudden—
   To take away poor people's breath?
Why, bless us, here's pork and pease-puddin',
   Till we both die a natural death.'

    *   *   *   *   *

'Seems strange that, among such a many,'
   Says Jerry, relaxing his grin,
'I can't find a pound or a penny——'
   'I've found a bad sixpence!' says Jinn.

'Not you,' said her husband. 'I've got it.
   It's just as I've often been told:—
This heap was all hoarded and potted
   By one of the Ancients of old.

'It seems they was thriving old fellers,
   With mortal more money than brains;
So some they locked up in their cellars,
   And some they let down in the drains.

'The gold's got a little bit mottled—
   Won't any way pass at the shop—
So, Jinn, let's again get it bottled,
   And clap on the stopper a-top.

'We must hide it, and keep it all snug, Jinn,
   So mind how you talk with your tongue.
If any one knew what I've dug, Jinn,
   My eyes! you'd be solemnly hung.'

'If lawyers do ever make law like
   The law that you mention,' Jinn said,
'They ought to be flown upon war-like,
   Or smothered all round in their bed.

'But that's not the question, provided
   I get my sweet Alderney cow.
Till then, how's the Jar to be hided?'
   Says Jerry—'The question is—how?

'There's the clothes-press, the copper, the cupboard,
   In which the concern we could stow.'
Cries Jinn—'If we come to be robbered,
   There's just where the foreman would go.

'I could bake it up hot in my oven—
   They'd blister their fingers and bray:
Or, if 'neath our bed it were shoven,
   We'd hear if they stole it away.'

Says Jerry—'I'd not give a stoat-scut
   In that kind o' case for my life!
We'd both of us wake with our throats cut,
   And find the Pot gone, little wife.'

'Good man! this is perfectly frightful!
   I wish it was back in the ground.
Let's both of us watch it from nightfall
   Till daylight begins to come round.'

'Agreed!' Through that long night in winter,
　　They heard the sharp centre-bits grind;
The door splitting splinter by splinter,
　　The cottage at last undermined.

They heard—you may fancy Jinn fainted—
　　The ringleader mutter and swear:
Till at last, when the skies were pink-painted,
　　They found—there'd been nobody there!

Why need the same tale be repeated?
　　Twelve nights the same torments they bore:
Twelve mornings, on darkness defeated,
　　They slued themselves round for a snore.

They breakfasted soon after seven,—
　　Or when it grew perfectly dark;—
They dined about half-past eleven,
　　And always drank tea with the lark.

Till neighbours, quite wild with amazement,
　　Invaded the garden of greens;
And flattened their beaks at the casement,
　　Surveying the softest of scenes.

'Gee-up! you two sleepy old people:
　　You've been a whole fortnight tucked in.
Hark, Jerry! there's noon by the steeple!
　　Whoop! wake up and tickle him, Jinn!'

'My friends,' came the voice of the Vicar,
　　'You really *must* be awoke.'
'A clear case of coma from liquor.'
　　The last was the Doctor who spoke.

'Break open the door,' cried the Justice;
  'The Coroner's wanted, I ween.
Good people, I charge you, assist us,
  In the name of our Lady the Queen!'

Crash!—There the kind couple lay sleeping—
  Their two noses touching—and, la!
Why, where do you think, for safe keeping,
  Slept swaddled and coddled—the Jar?

Don't ask me. The curtain domestic
  I hold should be sacredly spread.
'What's *this?*' cried the Justice majestic :—
  'A jorum of spirits, in bed?'

Up sprang Jinn and Jerry, and blended
  Their shrill sleepy voices aloud;
On finding their *levée* attended
  By such an inquisitive crowd.

'I did it. I'm guilty,' sobs Jerry;
  'I spaded it up like a thief.
If people such things go to bury,
  Of course they bring gardeners to grief.'

But, while they both clamoured and chattered,
  Again the Jar-stopper flew out;
And the floor was all sprinkled and scattered
  With gold that ran rolling about.

'Peace!' thundered that Justice egregious :
  'Good folks, this is matter of weight.
With villany dark and insidious,
  These traitors have struck at the State.

THE JAR OF GOLD.

'To jail must these Trovers of Treasure
  Be borne in the regular way;
And, during the Royal Displeasure,
  In jail these two Trovers will stay.

'Ay, Justice is not to be baffled:
  Serenely she poises her scales;
And points with her sword to the scaffold :—
  My clerk may discuss the details.'

'Your Worship'—with grave inclination
  Demurely made answer the clerk—
'Applauds, in sublime peroration,
  Those famous old Ages of Dark:

'When people hot fagots were stacked on,
  Or whipped at the end of a wain—
I mean when the late Mr. Bracton
  Had chambers in Chancery Lane;

'When to pick up a prize in your garden
  Was *contrà* the Royal Prerog.,
And sent you with small hope of pardon
  Away to Tyburnia to jog.

'But, had you so far condescended
  As further the theme to pursue,
You doubtless had spoke of laws mended,
  Till very much nicer than new.[1]

---

[1] His Worship's clerk appears to have had in his mind's eye at the moment the following letter :—

'WHITEHALL, *August* 27, 1860.

'SIR,—I am directed by the Secretary, Sir George Lewis, to inform you that the Lords Commissioners of the Treasury have been pleased

' Your Worship had probably added
 (Advice from your Worship's a gem),
The sooner these lucky folks padded
 To London, the better for them.

' Take train—then a cab to Whitehall, sir,
 And tinkle the Treasury bell :
The value of this—a fine haul, sir—
 Right out will the Government shell.

' No bad alteration, now, is it ?
 I fancy this fortunate pair
Had much better start on their visit
 Than cuddle away like that there.'

' Three cheers,' cried the Vicar, ' for Jerry !
 And three for his missis, my boys ! '
The place grew so awfully merry,
 You hardly could hear for the noise.

  *   *   *   *   *

to authorize the payment to finders of ancient coins, gold or silver ornaments, or other relics of antiquity, in England or Wales, of the actual value of the articles, on the same being delivered up for behoof of the Crown. And I am to request that you will instruct the police officers of your borough to give notice of the intentions of her Majesty's Government ; and to inform all persons who shall hereafter make discoveries of any such articles, that, on delivering them to the sheriff, they will receive from the Treasury rewards equal in value to the full intrinsic value of the articles.

 ' In all cases where it shall come to the knowledge of the police that such articles have been found, and that the persons having found them refuse or neglect to deliver them up, Sir George Lewis desires that measures may be taken for their recovery, and that information may be forwarded to him.,
     ' I am, Sir,
    ' Your obedient Servant,
      'GEO. CLIVE.

' *To the Chairman of the Watch Committee, York.*'

THE JAR OF GOLD.

No longer a clean little hovel
   Peeps meek from that garden of greens:
A villa now courts your approval,
   Supported by adequate means.

A beautiful Alderney grazes
   All day in the meadow close by;
While pigs, in their delicate phases,
   Give dutiful grunts from their sty.

But the best news of all is quite recent—
   A special performance of Jinn's—
Who, after an interval decent,
   Presented her husband with TWINS.

THE FLYING HORSE.

A LEAF FROM THE ARABIAN NIGHTS.

> 'There's something in a flying horse!'
> WORDSWORTH, *Prologue to Peter Bell.*

CANTO I.

THERE is a good old custom in the kingdom of Cashmere,
With flying flags and beating drums, to welcome in the year;
To set a gallant fair afoot, with spacious booths and gay,
And keep the merry Nevrouz-time, which we call New Year's day.

Not there the Fantoccini show—the tumbler on the cord—
The wax-work van—the Acrobats—the man that eats the sword—
The beer within the drinking booth—the pork upon the pole,
To glut the cockney appetite, and vulgarize the soul.

From all the wealthy provinces, the steady craftsmen bring
The best of all their workmanship to set before the king;
That he may judge their diligence, as proved in every stall;
Rebuke the bad, reward the good, and crown the best of all.

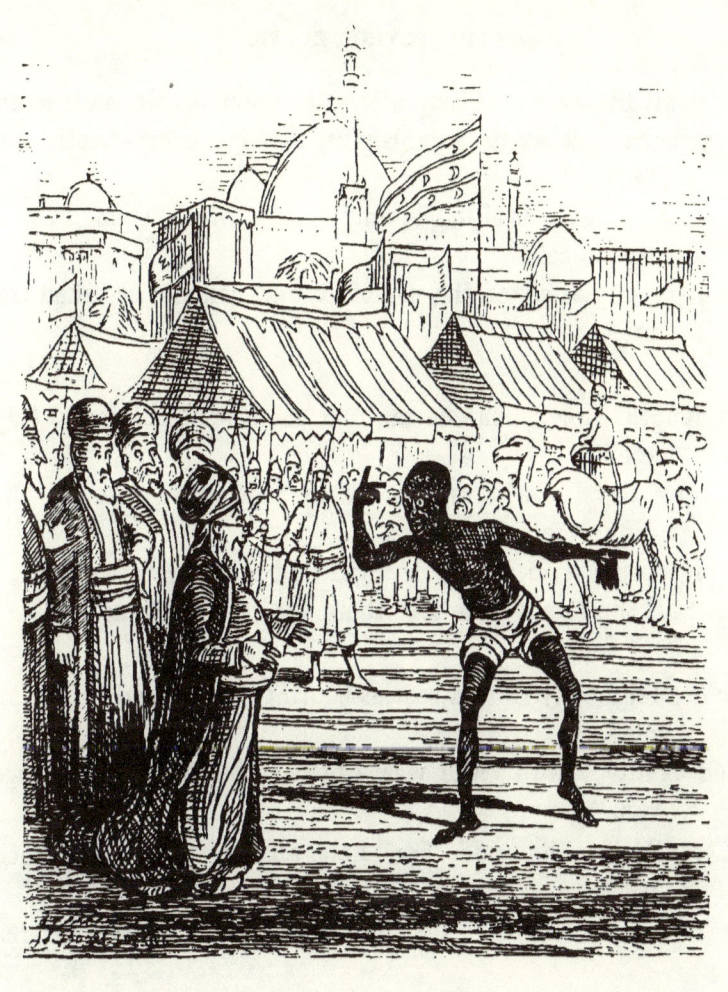

With all his court and councillors, the good old monarch went,
The morning that my tale begins, through every booth and
    tent:
He praised each well-made implement, with 'Come, that's
    very nice!'
And sometimes asked the use of it, and sometimes asked the
    price.

At length—for monarchs are but men—'Methinks a tidy
    spell,
A long day's work, my lords,' he said; 'Ho, sound th
    dinner-bell!
A pigeon-pie with sherry dry will find more grace with me,
Than all the "raw material" there yet remains to see.'

Then straightway from a scarlet booth there jumped an Indian
    man,
And boldly towards the weary prince the sun-black savage
    ran.
'Lor, King!' he said, 'me here all day from six o'clock
    till four,
In hopes to show you something dat you nebber seen before.

'Do come along—it won't be long: for if you will not wait,
To-morrow all de folks will say, de King him come too late;
Him nebber see de famous horse dat in de Indian stall:
Dis King no wise: him give no prize to what was best
    of all!'

'Dear me,' the good old monarch said, 'since you've so
    much to show,
And cannot wait, our spoon and plate awhile we must
    forego:

Lead on, my friend, and we'll attend : we praise your work-
    man zeal,
And hold the cause of Industry far dearer than our meal.'

Three summersaults that Indian cut, and chuckling led
    the way ;—
His apish face had not a trace of aught save craft and clay ;
The fire that shines through lips and eyes, and speaks the
    man within,
Had never yet been lighted in that swarthy child of sin.

    'Ah, bless my soul,' the good king said,
      'A model, I presume,
    Of steeds beyond the Tigris bred ?
      Confound him, where's my groom ?
    'Tis very clever—nice indeed !
      He looks almost alive ;
    Now, pray—a horse of such a breed
      Do people ride or drive ?
    Aha ! yes—thank you ! bless my heart,
      What a long way to send
    So very large a work of art ;
      Good day, my honest friend ! '

    'Stop, massa king,' the Indian cried,
      And flashed his coal-black eye ;
    'You tink my nag a straw-stuffed hide,
    Like what de piccanniny ride ;
      Dat neither kind nor sly.
    Look here ! I turn dis tiny peg,
    And up he lift his fine fore-leg,
      And swish dat silken tail !
    I turn it more—he stamp and snort—
    Ha ! shall I ride him round the court,
      And top a six-foot rail ?

Not I, indeed, for what the need
To praise or puff so rare a steed ?
   I tell you he can fly!
Turn but dat peg completely round,
He'll dash like arrow from the ground,
   And gallop in the sky!
You guide him straight with bridle rein,
You prance on cloud, you cross the main,
You see the stars extremely plain,
   Like pumpkins—only bigger.
You do much more—too fine to tell,
But dat's enough : me here to sell ;—
If, as I tink, you like him well,
   Perhaps you'll name your figure.'

'My lords—my lords!' exclaimed the King,
'Who ever saw so strange a thing,
   Or dreamt of such a horse?
Ha, ha! when turned the tiny peg
To see him lift his fine fore-leg!
   Buy him? of course—of course!
I would not for the five great zones,
The wealth of all their thousand thrones,
   This masterpiece of art
Should ever fill a gilded shrine
In other halls than these of mine,
   Or glad some rival's heart!'

Outspake the bland Exchequer lord,
   'O King, give what you will ;
The doubt is what you *can't* afford,
   Whilst I command the till!

Bid what you please, great master mine ;
  No faithful liege will grudge it ;
Or, if the sulky slaves repine,
  Leave me to cook the budget.'

'There—there!' cried the King,
  'How much must he bring?
You've only to speak for the guineas to ring!'

'Go—offer your cash to the bird on the wing!'
Sneered the horse-dealing savage : 'dat lark in the sky,
Would gold fetch him down to be baked in a pie?
"O tanky," he say, and O tanky, say I.
  Now, hearkee to me,
  Dis horse dat you see
Was made by three fellers much wiser than we!

  'Nine years they sat a-thinking,
    With hand upon the chin,
  Across the work-bench winking,
    Before they did begin.

  'Nine years they spent a-talking
    Of what their thoughts had been,
  In turn their plans a-chalking
    Upon the workshop screen.

  'Nine years they toiled a-building,
    And then they came to die ;
  Two graves, alas! were filled in
    Before the Horse would fly.

  'But when the last lay sickly,
    He kindly sent for me ;
  Says they, "My lad, come quickly
    He's almost up the tree!"

'I went: I found him dying;
   But he said, "The work is done.
The Horse that goes a-flying
   I leave to you, my son.
The secret's in a parchment scroll,
   Concealed within my breeches;
One promise, please:—upon your soul,
   You won't for filthy riches
Resign the prize: demand no less
   Of those who'll swarm to buy,
Than a respectable Princess;
   Good-bye, my lad—good-bye!"
Now, what you say? your daughter's nice;—
I'm not so nasty:—that's the price!'

You may guess that an offer so friendly and frank
Made the Court and the King look remarkably blank.
      Still it seemed so absurd,
      He thought, at a word,
To lose the fine Horse that could fly like a bird,
      That he didn't give way
      To his temper and say
Such horrid strong things as papas, in the play,
Would seem to consider give point to their 'nay.'
      He argued, 'This lout
      Knows what he's about;
There are more ways than one, though, to tickle a trout!
A wretch who can scarce know the clink of a ducat
Will jump at the offer of gold by the bucket;
While, as for my daughter—an impudent whim!
We'll try how diplomacy answers with him.

'Your Horse, my good friend—a mere toy though it be—
I wish to possess. In selecting your fee,

I must say you'd better have left it to me.
To sneer at hard cash, man, is humbug so rank
I doubt if you ever went over the bank;
To ask for my daughter is still more insane :—
Why, every one knows she's peculiarly plain;
   She squints with one eye,
   And one shoulder's too high,
And she hops in her walk;—she's a positive Guy!
And her hair's run to seed like a crop of dry teazles,
And, only last night, she broke out in the measles.
Of course, if you wish me, I'm ready to bid her
Accept you at once : don't be rash, but consider!'

   Then forth from the ring
   That surrounded the King,
The Prince Heir-Apparent advanced with a spring.
'Good gracious,' he shouted, 'to speak so of sister!
I'm sure it's a wonder your tongue doesn't blister!
This blubber-lipped rascal, this woolly-pate cur,
To dare to come here and talk nonsense of her!
And you, at your age too, to gape at his Horse,
As if the whole thing wasn't humbug of course!
If you must be convinced it's a thundering do,
Here!—I'm in the saddle, and round goes the screw!'

For my part—who never, I'm sorry to sing,
Could pull, without flinching, my shower-bath string—
I candidly own that his Highness's freak
Appears, to my thinking, both wilful and weak;
And, being by nature much wiser than witty,
Regard such a simpleton simply with pity.

With a great crash of clock-work and jingle of wheels,
The savage steed instantly kicked up his heels.

Gave a stamp and a bound and a plunge and a neigh,
Sprang snorting from earth and flew soaring away!
  Straight, straight through the air
  He rattled full tear,
Galloping, galloping goodness knows where!
Till the Prince, whom they followed with horrified stare,
Far dwindled in distance and ether quite thin,
Looked less than a walnut—a whitebait—a pin!
And, in five minutes more, so exceedingly small,
There really was nothing to look at at all!

'Ho! seize me the traitor—the fiend! he shall swing!
Odd's bomb-shells and catapults!' thundered the King.
'You gallows-faced heathen! how durst you draw nigh,
Thief—ape that you are! with a horse that could fly?
  Do you see what he's done!
  Flown away with my son!
That's all! O by Jove, but you'll pay for your fun!
Where is he? I ask you—you villanous black!
Is he lost? Is it likely the Horse will come back?'

'Sare, why speak to me? How you 'spect me to know
Where dis foolish young gentleman likely to go?
Me run up to stop him;—him tell me "get out!"
Me 'spostulate 'spectful;—him hit me a clout.
Me no time to show him de oder peg, sare,
Dat make de fine Horse come down out of de air.
If he no find it out, him continue to fly
Till him knock a great hole in de roof of de sky!
Me s'pose dat him get in de debbil's own row——'

'Cease, Traitor!' the King said: 'I solemnly vow
  That if, safe and sound,
  My boy isn't found,

Before the great sun has completed his round,
In twenty-four hours told off by the clock,
Our headsman shall hand you at once to the block.
What ho, Provost Marshal! clap chains by the ton—
Clap fetters—clap shots of a forty-pound gun
On elbow and ankle, and hammer like fun,
Till, this time to-morrow, we ask for our son!'

'Twere needless to tell what a frightful to-do
Upset the whole palace; how dreadfully blue
The 'Sticks' and the 'Grooms' and the chamberlains
    grew;
(As any good Stick would, of course, at the bare hint
That the Heir to the throne was no longer Apparent.)
How the King feeling anxious and wakeful—no wonder!
Lay winking and thinking and roaring like thunder;
While, chained in the cellar, that Indian perfidious
With yells made the night inconceivably hideous.
All this, which decidedly out of our line is,
We briefly pass over to follow his Highness.

    Away, away, through the pathless blue,
    Higher than ever the condor flew;
    Over the desolate mountain-height,
    Over the glacier jagged and white;
    Over the deep dusk plains beneath,
    Crossed by many a wandering wreath,
    Without one sound or mark of man
    Throughout their shadowy rounded span;
    Stretching away like a swarthy lea,
    To the luminous line of the distant sea.

    The very first words Prince Firouz spoke
    Were, 'Dash my luck, but it's past a joke!

A curse I say on my folly to back
This clattering, fly-away, clock-work hack!
I can't pull him in, for he's all made of tin,
And, to judge by the way the wheels jingle and spin,
He may fly for a week, and the pestilent pin
That started won't stop him; oh, murder! I see
In more ways than one that it's all up with me!'

Now, in cases like these—you may sneer if you please—
It's fifty times worse when you've no bread and cheese—
  And hence, as he flew
  Through the fast-falling dew,
Each supperless moment more frantic he grew;
And tugged at the bridle, and twisted the screw;
  Till down sunk the sun:
  I'm certain, for one,
He'd have pitched himself over as sure as a gun,
If, just at that moment, he hadn't espied
A second small handle, deep sunk in the hide.
'Thank Heaven, at last there's a chance to be tried!
I can't be worse off—that's a comfort!' he cried;
'Even if—as most likely—'tis part of the trick,
And you screw up *this* peg when you want him to kick.'

  No!—down at the touch
  Went the steed very much
Like a crow on a fallow slow-sinking, and such
Was the giddy sensation as wheeling and wheeling
He went, that the Prince lost all thinking and feeling,
And found all his brain-work as quickly congealing
As if playing pendulum, legs to the ceiling.

  Starting at last, as out of a dream,
  He woke to find the clear moon shining
  Full on his face:—' Well, don't it seem,'
  He said, ' as if I *had* been dining?

But no—I'm as sober as sober may be ;
And I don't see a hedge and I don't see a tree—
A roof as I live ! I *am* pleasantly planted !
Adventures for ever—no doubt I'm enchanted.
What's yonder ? a Horse by all the fates,
Insanely trying to graze off the slates !
Bah ! fool that I am—I remember it all !
He's back upon earth to look out for a stall.
Nice place too, confound him, he's found for his drop,
Where all's topsy-turvy—and I'm on the top !
Hope I shan't smash in a manner most horr'ble,
Trying to shin my way down to the door-bell ! '

   After infinite groping
   Round roof-top and coping,
He reached a dark nook, where a ladder went sloping,
By way of a species of airy back-stair,
One couldn't for certain prognosticate where.

  An endless terrace carved and laid
   With snow-bright marble : not a sound,
  Nor sign—save where the moonlight played
   Along what seemed enchanted ground,
  And on the three great windows bright,
  Flung open to the sultry night.

  From slowly-burning lamps within,
  Creeps on the air a golden gloss,
   The giddy bats fly blindly in,
  Through floating trailers looped across :
   And out again, on soundless wing,
  They dive and flit the platform round ;
   But hark ! whose jingling footsteps ring ?
  Who dares to tread enchanted ground ?

'Aha!' cried the Prince,
'This is charming, but since
I'm rather too hungry the matter to mince,
I'll just beg a peep through those curtains of chintz!
The windows would hardly be open so wide,
I should think, if one wasn't expected inside.
Ha! beauty, by jingo!'—
      So still she sate
  Amid the grand armorial panes
 Flung backward from her chair of state,
  You might have deemed that from her veins
All force had ebbed, as if to rise
Resistless in those noble eyes.

Half leaning on the faultless arm,
 That shone through glossy waves of hair,
She sat, the spirit of the calm,
 The Queen of Moonlight, gazing there:
Gazing on the grand procession,
 Brightly marching east and west;
Star and planet's thick succession,
 Toiling orbs that scorn at rest!

Hair-brained was the Prince and reckless,
 But his face due qualms expressed,
When he saw the diamond necklace
 Throbbing on her startled breast;
And when she, with calm impatience,
 Queen-like eyes upon him fixed,
Then, indeed, his young sensations
 Grew at once extremely 'mixed;'
Not that she looked annoyed or furious,
But much surprised, and proudly curious.

'I'm the Prince of Cashmere.'

'I'm the Child[1] of Bengal.'

'I'm intruding, I fear.'—

'Oh, dear, not at all !
But our ditches are deep and our walls are high,
And our warders are fierce and let nobody by,
And you didn't, I fancy, drop down from the sky !'

'I fancy I did,'
Said the Prince ; 'but pray bid
Your cook to peep under his pudding-pot lid !
I swear I'm so hungry I'd feed off a horse,
Without making faces or asking for sauce !'—

'Dear me—dear me !' said the sweet Princess,
'How shocking ! some supper he quickly shall dress ;
Your fork you shall stick in
The wing of a chicken,
And revel in salad that lobster shall thicken ;
Champagne shan't be wanting to fill up a chink,
Nor punch that would make a dried crocodile wink ;
So few are our visitors here in Bengal,
I'm only too pleased you came this way to call.'

Delightful days ! I've often thought,—
Before this grand old world spun steady ;
When life was all with freshness fraught—
No tale had yet been told already.
When folks had little else to do
But smoke their pipes in gardens rosy ;
Till mild adventures came to woo,—
Certain to end in something cosy.

[1] Pro 'Infantâ,' scilicet Princess,—prosodiæ gratiâ.

Ah, well-a-day ! so, times there were
   Of which some honest Saurian
Delivered us from further care
   By swallowing the historian:
When wriggling out of old-world eggs,
   Came huge land-lubber whales,
With fourscore eyes and fifty legs
   And several dozen tails;
When sprawled fat spiders, yards across,
   And each primæval lizard
Could grind a tough rhinoceros
   Alive within his gizzard.
Till Time came by with sand and scythe,
   To banish the colossal;
And pitched their naked bones to writhe
   In gaunt museum-fossil;
Long may they rest in idle truce,
   Quartz-coffined and age smitten,
Who'd wish to see a mammoth loose,
   His best friend bruised and bitten?
But must all eras change alike,—
   The same coarse hand crush all?
The steel that should the elm-tree strike,
   On bleeding violets fall?
And could not even Time forbear
   To spoil those charming days,
Whose very sunset in the air
   Still gilds Arabia's lays?

    Now, honest old wall!
    I prithee tell all
That met the sweet ears of the Child of Bengal;
How spoke the gay Prince at the blithe *tête-à-tête*,
That grew so imprudently lengthy and late?

'Ah, royal Child!'—(I give the pith,)
  'Since life within me rallied,
(Another tumbler, hot, please, *with* :—
  This is indeed a salad!)
Your beauty's done its work on me,
  And heaven be my witness,
Without your smiles the world would be,
  (Oh, what a plate of kidneys!)
I say the world were one wide blank,
  A hopeless hateful prison;
(Such glorious punch I never drank!)
  My angel, won't you listen?'

Then, shifting down from love to gold,
  His father's wealth he sounded;
His fame in fifty books enrolled,
  His realm almost unbounded.
He talked of chested millions,
  Of pearl tiaras ten,
Of crimson war-pavilions,
  And endless lanes of men.
Of sparkling palace-parapets
  That blazed a furlong high;
Fish-pools and flying fountain-jets
  That sprinkled half the sky!

Well pleased the lady listened
  To the sounding of such fame,
And her dark eyes brightly glistened
  When the wild proposal came:
But the Horse upon the house-top
  Made her start a little, too;
'For goodness' sake, sir, *now* stop!'
  She said; 'that *can't* be true!

What! gallop here from far Cashmere
   Along the yielding sky,
And reach Bengal ere night could fall!'

'You really wish to try?'
The Prince cried: 'Step upon the roof,
   Fair Child, and you shall see;
And find in this the clearest proof
   That you may trust in me.
You'll come? Brave girl, I knew it!
   Yon vault is not so dark
But he'll bear you safely through it,
   Till you hear the dog-star bark.
I now no longer fear him;
   I can curb his clock-work flight,
And I know the way to steer him,
   So mind you hold me tight!'

   *   *   *   *

Aslant Cashmere the morning breaks, and grows to sultry
   day;
Now from the brazen arch of noon, the cruel sunbeams play;
Now, striking from the purple west, they float in painted
   lines;
Now, round and rayless ere he sinks, the feeble monarch
   shines.

All day the King had stumped about, and asked of every one,
'Pray can you tell me anything of my departed son?'
Of course his worst misgivings would nobody avow,
So all they did for answer was to shake their heads and bow.

Then mad with wrath and fear he grew, and ill with rage of
   mind;
'Bring forth,' he said, 'this Indiaman; this cunning
   knave unbind;

Set out the block and basket, that his head may grin
    to-night
Upon the steepest pinnacle that crowns our palace height!'

Out came the solemn headsman, with his heavy, shouldered
    axe;
Out came the wretched Indian, whining, 'Bless me! what
    a tax
To pay for bringing here a horse which, it must be allowed,
Whips all the world for workmanship!' 'Speak up, sir!'
    bawled the crowd.

    The headsman swings his hatchet
        Three times aloft in air :—
    To see the nigger catch it,
        The people press and stare.

'Hold, hold the death-stroke—hearken!
    The Prince—the Prince! hooray!'
Caps, flung by thousands, darken
    At once the face of day.
'Hooray, our fine young master,
    He's here all safe and sound!
There isn't no disaster!'
    Roar all the folks around.

'Hug, hug me, Royal Father!
    A lady on the crupper!
She loves me too, sir—rather!
    And, oh! sir, such a supper!
Such kidneys! oh! such lovely eyes,
    And such a little waist!
She's here—no there, sir, in disguise,
    For fear she should be chased!'

'Dear me, dear me,' the monarch said, 'I don't quite
    comprehend :
Pray where were you the livelong night?—and who's your
    female friend?
I don't quite see the story's point, or why she should be
    chased,
You skip so quick from kidneys to the lady's little waist!'

Again the frank young Prince began and told the story
    through,
Commencing where, aloft in air, the mad sky-charger flew.
He prosed about the charming Child, a little, to be sure,
And sketched, with pardonable pride, his brilliant *coup
    d'amour*.

    'I chose not that the million
      Should say,' continued he,
    '"He came a riding pillion,
      With a wife upon his knee;"
    And therefore I alighted
      At our country palace gate,
    Till, royally invited,
      I bring her home in state.
    Pursuit! a likely notion!
      I'm not myself, sir, yet;
    That nag's confounded motion
      Might steadier brains upset.'

'Ah, that reminds me,' cried the King. 'Why, bless my
    heart and soul,
They're cropping off the rascal's head to clap upon a pole;
He needn't die—of course not—if you're certain you're
    alive—
Quick! stay his fate, and through the gate that hateful
    heathen drive!

'And, for a hint, let kicks imprint their postscript full astern,
That lightly of the lame-foot maid [1] the tingle he may learn.
Now, lovelorn son, this mercy done, we'll view your lady's charms;
Ho! turn a torch-light escort out, and drummers beat to arms!'

Danced on the drum the 'larum loud, the clear-throat bugles blew;
Its ravel bright of roaring light each bursting bonfire threw;
Forth strode the milk-white elephants in huge throne-laden pairs,
And, shuddering at their footfall weight, far shook the city squares.

Then down the crowded rampart-line a cheer like thunder ran,
As through the massive gateway-arch poured the long-lighted van;
As rose amid the roar of drums the stormy serenade,
And streaming down the causeway went the endless cavalcade.

The fleece-drawn mist hangs bloodshot o'er the torchmen's winding line;
Like shock-hair'd goblins of the dew the palm-trees blink and shine;
Till breeze-borne floats the wedding-march, blown back in filmy strains,
From a dusk-red hazy glimmer moving o'er the moonless plains.

[1] 'Pede Poena claudo.'

They tapped the Indian on the back,
   'Begone, you thief!' said they:
'You just make track, and don't come back,
   Or else alive you'll flay!
So swears his Royal Highness,
   And his word he's like to keep;
So don't abuse his kindness
   Now he's let you off so cheap.'

Uprose the kneeling victim
   With a scowl of serpent-hate,
And, as if the fiend had kicked him,
   Ran yelping through the gate.
You cannot think how cunning
   Was that varlet's foxy soul,
Nor, if you'd seen him running,
   Had you ever guessed his goal.
With horrid croaks of malice,
   And thoughts too vile to tell,
He reached the country palace,
   And briskly rang the bell.

'De Master of de Horse am I,'
   Said he, 'de King's a-coming;
Look where dat heap o' torches fly,
   And harkee to de drumming!
To seat upon de saddle
   His lady bright and true,
Young massa bid me rattle,
   Like a swish-tail kangaroo.
For, says he, "The crowd's quite fur'us
   To see my Princess fair,
And I guess they'll count it cur'us
   If I fetch her home by air!"

But what's the good o' talkin'
    Till we catch it 'cross the hide?
Will you please to let me walk in,
    Till I set the gal astride?'

Alas, too trusting beauty!
    Your Prince is at the gate;
But the nigger saves his booty
    And the bridegroom comes too late.
Alas, too sanguine lover,
    Dismounting at the doors!
As a pheasant whirrs from cover,
    Away the Indian soars!
Aloft a blazing flambeau
    He waves in triumph wild;
While, in the clutch of Sambo,
    Screams the affrighted Child!

'Hoy, Massa Prince—good-bye, sare!
    Dis nigger up to snuff!
You catch me? O you try, sare!
    Dat just one leetle tough.
Me nebber had de measles,
    So your sister count for small;
I'se one of dem born weasels
    You don't trap every fall!
Dis fine gal suit me better,
    All royal top to toe :—
Wal—in hopes to get a letter
    'Fore long, up sky we go!'

CANTO II.

Through curls of smoke
The morning broke
On every looming mountain-crown ;
But fiery fast,
Above them passed
The steed that sped from Cashmere town.

The horrible negro laughed with glee,
　As under them tossed and flew
The rough white foam of the China sea ;
　And he shouted a wild halloo
　　To the crew of a junk
　　That were howling with funk,
　As it wallowed a mastless wreck ;
　　And burning pastilles,
　　In piteous appeals
　To a corpulent Idol on deck.

'Twas noon by the sun,
Ere, gloomy and dun,
The forests of strange Japan
Rose out of the sea ;
' Now, harkee to me,
Young gal !' the nigger began :—
' Dat howlin's quite horrid, and 'tain't no good !
Don't holler, they say, till you're out of the wood ;
Wal now—of all woods dat I ever come near
Down yonder's the last where you'd make people hear,
　'Cause nobody lived there—never !

Dere's nothin' but monkeys and green cockatoos,
You can 'splain it all clear to 'em, course, if you choose,
   But it don't seem worth your endeavour.
It's plum in the middle I mean to pitch ;
   How happy my pet will be,
In her neat little wigwam of hickory switch,
   A-sitting on Sambo's knee :
      With nothin' to do
      De honeymoon through,
But fondle him nicely, and tell him how true
She loves him all down from de crown to de shoe !
Dere's cocoa-tree milk for her drink so sweet,
Dere's heaps of nuts for missy to eat ;
      De little buzz-bee
      Live top of de tree,
Me scramble to fetch her down honey for tea :—
      Here :—dis a good place
      To light from our race ;
Now missy—give Sambo a kiss on de face.'

   Indignant from the horse's back
     The proud young Princess sprang,
   And smote the nigger such a crack
     That his ebony jawbones rang.
     ' Wretch ! stand aside ! '
     She sternly cried ;
   ' Black poodle-headed thief !
   I, such a devil's nut-fed bride !
   Not if as many threats he tried
     As corn-seeds in the sheaf !
   Stand off ! beware the tiger-taught—
     The daughter of Bengal ! '

   ' Come ! none of dem 'ere tricks of court,
     Dey don't suit here at all,'

The ruffian said—'dere's time enough;
  Me just go rind a stick :—
If missy still cut up so rough,
  High time dis gal to lick!
Ha! wat dat sound? dat never come
  From any bird I know!
'Pears like a screamer cotched in gum;
  Ha! cuss! what bugles blow?'

He'd hardly spoke when horse and hound
  Came crashing through the wood,
With yelp and bound and bugle-sound,
  Towards where the lady stood.
The foremost on a raven steed,
  A square-set peppery man,
Was yet, as well the Child could read,
  The Lord of all Japan.
For I have heard and count for true,
  That royal eyes can tell
Their equals all disguises through,
  Such grace in kings doth dwell.

The monarch reined his raven steed,
  And raised his hunting-cap;
'Can aid so sweet a Princess need?
  Or what auspicious hap
Brings one so lovely to Japan,
  Where strangers touch so seldom?
And who—why, gallows take the man!
  Is that unwashed he-beldam?'

She could not speak—she only sprung
  And clasped him round the knee;
Her frightened eyes and cheeks all hung
  With tears were sad to see.

   ' Wat's dis ? ' the filthy negro cried ;
   ' How dare you, sare ! dis gal's my bride !
   Go 'long, you ole varmin,
   Trot back to your farmin',
'Cause, look you, I'm goin' to whip her a sarmin ;
   She wants it most precious,
   She's regular vicious :
I reckon I'll break her in raal judicious :—
   I'll make her flesh creep !
   I flog mighty deep—
I do, when I'm dandered : I'll hurt her a heap.
Ho, gal ! strip up ready— ! '
        One scimetar-sweep,
And the ravisher rolled in the grass like a sheep !
He kicked up his heels and he turned up his eyes,
And in short, as they say in the Tragedy, [*dies.*]

Alas, now I think of it,—Horace declares
Bad people should always be killed below-stairs :
And that ever, for fear the discerning should criticise,
Rank blood you should carefully curtain from Pity's eyes.
He's right, I confess. I was wanting in tact.
Henceforward, all skulls shall be privately cracked.

Need I formally state, at so gory a sight,
How Mademoiselle fainted off-hand in a fright ;
How they tickled her, splashed her, and ripped up her
  stays,
And tried, but in vain, her sweet eyelids to raise,
Till, finding that never a word she spoke,
And nought they could think of the lady awoke,
They carried her home on a horseman's cloak.

Gazed on the Courser, in puzzle and fume,
Monarch and equerry, huntsman and groom.

Gravely impassive, the deep agate eye
Calmly contracted and closed in reply !
    So awful a wink,
    So sepulchral a clink—
Like the sound of a gong gone alive down a sink—
Startled and shocked these poor children of venery ;
Fond of their woods, and unused to machinery.

To the Royal Museum at last in despair,
The strange, imperturbable mammal they bare.
    Over his 'card'
    Savans fought hard ;
Doubted and scouted and shouted and sparred,
In language a great deal too bad for a bard ;
And so the discussion at once I discard,
    To copy the ticket
    Pinned on his picket :—

Icthus Gelastos

(Queer Fish from our Thicket).

A broad and royal chamber,
    The dawn-light slanting in,
Through panes of Orient amber,
    As if one smile to win ;
One waking smile from her who lies—
Deep sleep upon those curtained eyes !

    Around her fragrant pillow,
      A bower of plumes and gold
    Droops like a glittering willow ;
      And still in slumber's fold,

She stirs not though the sunbeams, now,
Have trembling kissed her queenly brow.

Hark! trumpets in the palace court,
   Their clear and gay réveillée flinging;
And bang! the cannon from the fort
   Set all the pictured windows ringing,
And roar to all the tower bells
   To loose their clamorous tongues to-day:—
She wakes at last, as hoarsely swells,
   Down street and square, one grand 'hooray!'

Around her couch a maiden train
   On bended knees present their duty,
Yet lavish all their airs in vain
   Upon the dark-eyed southern beauty.
She gazes round in strange surprise;
   'Where am I? was it all a dream?
The Prince—the Indian?' 'Bless your eyes,
   He loves you as a cat loves cream!
He does indeed, ma'am,' chirp they all;
'You'll meet him in the Peacock Hall!'

'Meet whom?' she asks; 'whose halls are these?
   What boisterous mirth is yonder, pray?
What guns and bells?' 'Oh dear, ma'am, please
   Remember 'tis your wedding day!
They say his Highness did not sleep
   One mortal wink the livelong night;
And twice upon the floor did leap,
   Each time exclaiming, "Hold me tight!
Don't let me dart her dreams to break!"
Ah! what a husband, miss, he'll make!'

What bondage is rhyme! Why, just here I'd lay down
A large sum of money—to wit half a crown,
To be loose for five minutes and tell you in prose
What grief in the Child's pretty bosom arose;
What thoughts of the Prince! O, it's cruelly hard
To shamble along like a handicapped bard,
While three-volume tinkers plod recklessly by :—
No Abbey for them, though—no, no! when they die!

A sad fix was hers, because Kings of the East
Don't stand upon trifles—in courtship at least;
And boldly condense all the usual twaddle
To 'will you, or won't you? a nod or a noddle?'
She felt that to stave off her destiny sad,
But one way was open—at once to sham mad.

Each moment was precious :—she slapped her maids' faces,
Let fly, fore and aft, all her loops and her laces;
And then—kicking handsomely over the traces—
Sang out for a pipe and a bottle of rum,
And finished by savagely sucking her thumb.

Dumbfoundered, her horrified handmaidens ran
For the chief palace doctor—a learned young man.
He came—put the usual questions, 'for luck,'
She gave him no answer, but quacked like a duck :
That settled the business : 'Alas, it's too plain!'
He muttered—' Her Highness is clearly insane ;
My questions are all so provokingly parried,
I doubt but she's even too mad to be married!'

Bright burned the King's anger on learning the state
Of one he'd been pleased to select as a mate.

Gloomily growling he stalked to and fro,
With his hands in his pockets as far as they'd go,
Then sent for the doctor—'I wish you to know,'
Said he, 'if the lady's not well in a week,
Your neck it's our royal intention to tweak:
It's just kill or cure, man, and perfectly fair;
I like to be candid, so Bolus beware!'

Poor Bolus went out with a terrified squint,
Right sorely dismayed at this practical hint;
He bled her, he cupped her—blue bottles and red
Prescribed without ceasing, and blistered her head;
In short, all the orthodox changes were rung,
Till the end of the week: and then Bolus was hung.

The cry was, 'More doctors!' More doctors there came,
But signally failed the young lady to tame;
And daily some leech, as the patient grew worse,
Who called in his carriage, drove home in a hearse.

Enraged at such failures, his Majesty then
Demolished the Hall of those medical men.
To jail went the College;—their ears were all clipped,
They were privately blistered, and publicly whipped:
Each day, at the hands of the hangman, they quaffed
A fine, frothy goblet of double black-draught;—
'The discipline's rough, but the fault is your own,'
Said the King, 'I must raise your professional tone.'

As a final resource, he bade Heralds proclaim,
Through all the wide land, in his Majesty's name:—
'Volunteers to the front! Any bold amateur,
Who fancies he's able the Princess to cure,
May drop in and do it. In case of success,
Her weight in pure gold will but faintly express

Our sense of his merit. In case he should mull it,
We shall weigh him himself—with a rope round his gullet.'

* * * * * * *

'But how about the luckless Prince?'
   I hear some reader say;
'Pray what has *he* been doing since
   The Indian soared away?

'Perhaps he sought an early grave,
   From youth's bright hopes debarred;
Or did he simply stamp and rave?
   Out with it, master Bard!'

   I'll tell you. On first
   Comprehending the worst,
The yells he sent after that Indian accurst
   Were something quite awful;
   Indeed such a jaw-full
Of terms that in Bow Street are voted unlawful,
And cheap at five shillings, you'd really have thought
He couldn't in youth have been properly taught.
On cooling, however, he clearly perceived,
That thus the lost maiden would ne'er be retrieved;
And wisely remarked, 'If the Child I can't follow,
At least she shan't think that my love is all hollow;
But follow I will!'
                In those days, you should know,
Mere gentlefolks didn't a travelling go:
No cockney had ever yet ventured a stroll
On the banks of the Rhine, or beheld the Tyrol.
Club-Alpine's bold sons, had they lived at the time,
Would have scaled Shooter's Hill when in want of a climb,

Or, may be, indulged in a heart-broken moan
For Albion's white cliffs on the beach at Boulogne ;
At present our troubles are sorely increased,
When each travelled monkey tells tales of the East.

In short, it was everywhere quite understood,
A tourist, as such, could be after no good.
A pilgrim passed freely, and so did a pedlar,
But every one else was a ' spy ' or a ' meddler.'

Our hero accordingly purchased a ' pack '—
Brushed his hat the wrong way, turned his shirt-collars back,
Put a pipe in his mouth and his gloves in his pocket—
And went to a general dealer's to stock it.

No curious reader will ask me, I hope,
For a formal detail of the ribbons and soap,
Rouge, tweezers, tin thimbles, pills, hair-dyes, and snuff,
Which made his great wallet look handsome enough ;
Suffice it to say—that convenient old phrase !
The Prince drove away in a bagman-like chaise ;
And caring but little where Fortune might lead,
Like honest Don Quixote, left that to his steed.

   Towards the end of the day,
   He reached a great bay,
Where lay a stout Indiaman bound for Cathay ;—
   The Captain was bawling,
   The sailors were hauling,
Or flourishing, shoreward, their hats of tarpauling ;—
' May be,' cried the Prince, ' these fine fellows will fall in
With her whom I seek ! I'll at once volunteer ;
'Twill be fifty times better than snivelling here !'

He did.   Says the mate, 'You young shaver, avast!
You must mind how you haul or you'll fetch down the
        mast!
You Little Boy-blue!   Why, what good are you?
No matter, go for'ard! we're short of our crew.
If you don't pull your pound, lad, you dance at the gangway,'
He added, and swore a good deal in a slang way,
With divers allusions to 'timbers' and 'eyes,'
That shore-keeping readers would rather surprise,
And made—though they wouldn't be pretty to read—
The Prince go below, very nervous indeed.

Some weeks had gone by since that fine afternoon,
When down on their course came a frightful typhoon.
It roared through the rigging and thrashed them about,—
The mate had his eyelids blown clean inside out,
The bulwarks were stove, and the water washed in,
Till the men at the pumps were all up to the chin;
In short, to save life—they could hope for no more—
They put the helm up, and so ran her ashore.

The Prince, who instinctively snatched up his pack,
When he found all the timbers beginning to crack,
(At such dreadful times, as you've probably read,
The queerest of fancies come into one's head,)
Reached land on a grating; but scarcely had set
His foot on hard ground, before, sneezing and wet,
He was pounced upon, pummelled, and gagged like a felon,
With outrages perfectly painful to dwell on;—
         'Now, listen, young man,
            Your foot's in Japan!'
They shouted, 'Ah! get it away if you can!
Come, try it at once, for you've no time to spare;
It's not so much longer that noddle you'll wear!'

They led the wretched youth away
    Before a pig-tailed ' beak ;'
' Now, stranger, hast thou aught to say ?
    If so, you'd better speak !
Our laws are death to those who land
    Within these isles of ours ;
It seems they caught you on the strand—
    A Pedlar by the powers !
Unstrap his pack from off his back,
    And what the wares may be
That brought him thus to trade with us,
    We'll very quickly see !
Ha ! snuff and tobacco :—a smuggler, I'll swear !
Rouge, tweezers, tin thimbles !—hem ! dyes for the hair !
And, hollo ! see, ' Holloway's Ointment and Pills,
The Only Infallible Cure for All Ills !'
O, ho ! that explains it ! I now see it all !
He's after that blessed young Child of Bengal !
Did you come, my young friend, to effect her recovery ? '

' I did !' screamed the Prince. " I'm her slave, I'm her lover, I
Came to recover her ! Oh, is she here ?'

' Not so fast,' growled the Magistrate, looking severe :—
' If that be your object, the King's Proclamation
Commands us to pass you without molestation ;
But hark ye ! they tell me the lucky man's fee
The weight in pure gold of that lady will be !
One-half, my gay pill-box, is ample for *you ;*
The rest must reward me for letting you through :
Should you ever return, with your head on its socket,
Remember, I've that little claim on your pocket !'

Albeit the Prince was puzzled sore,
   He wisely answered, ' Done !
When next we meet on yonder shore,
   We halve the gold I've won :
Meanwhile, I'd thank your Lordship
   To make my bearings clear,
For, as we say aboard ship,
   I don't see how to steer.'

    *   *   *   *

The palace gates are gained at last,
The drawbridge cleared—the sentries passed :
' From foreign lands across the sea,
I come to work a cure,' said he ;
' Where is the lady ? show me in,
And let the charm at once begin.'

Outspake the palace-porter,
   A very friendly man,
' To come across the water
   Was but a simple plan,
Because you might have died at home,
Nor ever braved the roaring foam.

' Yon skulls that peel and blister
   In the sweltering noon-day sun
Could not one bit assist her,
   But came off one by one :
Ay, all you doctors fare alike,
There won't be soon one empty spike.

' Between the homœopathist,
   Who grins there on the right,
And yon poor damp hydropathist,
   Who only died last night,

Your head will hang to-morrow morning ;—
Ah—well! if you will take no warning,—
Go in and welcome : that's the door.
And there's the lady, on the floor!'

'Fly, Doctor!' cried the Princess—'fly!
I can't be cured : it's vain to try!
Hence, pounder, with your pills and pack!
I'm mad—I know it! quack, quack, quack!
Don't stay, I charge you on your life!
I'll never be the monster's wife!
What, linger still?——Good gracious, yes!
I know him in his pedlar's dress!
My darling Prince! I am so glad!
No, dearest, I'm not really mad!'

Quite needless were it to persist
   In tearing from such scenes the veil;
The 'happy couple' hugged and kissed,
   No doubt—but that's beside my tale :
'I do not rhyme to that dull elf,'
Who never did such things himself.

As quick as pigeons on the wing,
Her maidens ran to find the King;
'Oh, Sire!' they clamoured, 'please come quick;
A Pedlar's been and done the trick!
At once they both a-kissing fell,—
And kissing seems to make her well!'

In rushed the King—'Your hand, my friend!
The means which led to such an end
We will not question! There's your cheque ;—
Remember that we've spared your neck;

Our banker's gone abroad, but, dash it—
It's odd if somebody won't cash it;
Till then, you see, you've less to carry:—
And now, my Queen, at once we'll marry!'

    Confounded stood the lovers;
      But the royal Pedlar said,
    ' Until she quite recovers
      It were not safe to wed:—
There's magic been at work on her,
      That hasn't run its course;
'Twas drawn, unless I greatly err,
      From an Enchanted Horse!
I only wish I had it here,
      I'd soon set matters right;
And then your Highness needn't fear
      To marry her to-night.'

' To be sure!' cried the King;
  ' Now you mention the thing,
We picked up a nag that they hither shall bring.
And then cut your conjuring short, by the bye;
I hate being treated like Christopher Sly!'

The Horse, as I mentioned, I think, had been placed
In the Royal Museum; where canons of taste
Made them lock all ' hobgoblin-like' goods out of sight,
In a snug shady ' basement,'[1] that suited them quite:
And hence his good looks were a trifle gone by,
Being mouldy, and *minus* a tail and an eye.

---

[1] See *Quarterly Review*, Art. 'British Museum,' vol. clxxv. p. 153.

'Draw him forth,' said the Prince, 'to the principal square :
Out, guard, with drums beating and bayonets bare !
Swing censers all round him ;—stand back, if you please ;
The lady must mount him and sit at her ease :
More incense, more incense ! continue to smoke us,
Whilst I disenchant her ! now then,—Hokus pokus !
And presto, away !'
                              To the saddle he sprang,
The fizzing horse-clock-work went round with a clang :—
' Hurrah for check-mate ! My fine fellow, you're done !
So, next time your thoughts upon marrying run,
Be wise and don't act like an owlish old Cadi,
But previously ask the consent of the lady !'

All right-minded people will hear with delight
That the lovers arrived at Cashmere before night ;
The wedding went off with the greatest *éclat*,
The Prince on the throne soon replaced his papa ;
The Great Mogul dying, his daughter came in
For the throne of the Indies—the crown and the tin ;
And, all over Asia, their splendour and fame
Were every one's theme, till John Company came !

CAPTAIN TINDERBOX.

A TALE IN THREE VOLUMES.

Vol. I.

TOGGED in blue monkey, with buttons of brass;
Topped with tarpaulin-hat shining like glass;
Telescope tucked *à la fusil de chasse;*
Tipping his wink to each nurserymaid lass;
Trim little chip of a seafaring class;
Thus might you see Captain Tinderbox pass;
  With blithe little hum,
  Like a fiddle and drum,
'The Captain is coming—the Captain is come!'
(Our boatmen put words to his rum-tity-tum.)
'I'm happy,' he often would say, 'as a lord,
And that's why I keep the band playing aboard.'

  His age was unknown—
  Say forty, full-blown;
He'd weathered the weather in every known zone:
  Had broiled in the Tropic,
  Where warmth misanthropic
Makes free perspiration the principal topic;

  Had quaked in the Polar,
  Where colder and col'er
Folks wax in default of amenities solar;
  And—perils all past
  Of breaker and blast—
Had safe in the Temperate anchored at last.

Some people live lucky—some (just the reverse)
Seem born to misfortune that clings like a curse;
  And, do what they will,
  With care or with skill,
So surely the sugar-plum turns to a pill,
The sunshine to shade, and the sherry to squill,
The bonny bank-note to a creditor's bill.

Our Captain was one of these mortals unblest;
No ship he commanded arrived as addressed:
The first—a fine clipper—exploded off Brest.
  I'm told he was heard,
  As he circled and whirred
Through the air, giving orders as bright as a bird;
But that you know's humbug, of course, and absurd.

  A second ship came
  To grief much the same:
They say that again he showed infinite game,
And stuck to his post when surrounded with flame,
Impartial as ever in praise and in blame;
But people at Lloyd's put a mark to his name.

  And when the third broke
  Into volumes of smoke,
And the Captain, though perfectly ready to choke,
Gave cheer after cheer till the last was a croak,

It only seemed owners the more to provoke,
And no one thenceforward the Captain bespoke.

   So, stranded at last,
   Ashore hard and fast,
Our Captain his hours of idleness passed
At a sweet little place with a neat little quay,
Which is marked on the map as St. Mark's-on-the-sea.

   How he came by his cash
   I'd not be so rash
As even one single conjecture to flash;
But certain it is that he cut quite a dash—
   Built a trim little cot,
   With a tiny grass-plot,
And walks made of pebbles like six-pounder shot,
And a flagstaff in front, and an oyster-shell grot,
Surmounted by swivels, marines, and what not,
And cosily there made the most of his lot.

Boatmen and fishermen held him in awe;
Coastguard allowed him to lay down the law:
Good Mr. Maldon—the lord of the inn—
Crinkled and bowed on accepting his fin,
And all the small boys made no end of a din,
With cheering and 'Chuck us a penny, Old Tin!'

   'Twas a thing to behold,
   As each morning he strolled
On the pier of St. Mark's, how he pleased young and old
   To note the reply
   Of 'Cap'n, ay, ay!'
When something amiss had offended his eye,
And he shouted like thunder at once to know why.

To hear him, with telescope sweeping the rim,
Tell each passing sail by her tackle and trim;
Translate the sky-signals of Heaven, whose meaning
Too often is told when good ships are careening,
The tempest a-thrashing and devil a-gleaning;
Or else, by a circle attentive surrounded,
Not only read yesterday's *Times*, but expound it.

  Now, Stiggins, aroint!
  What need pry and point,
Or tell how Old Tin would his nightcap anoint?
  How no one could pass
  His cot but, alas!
Uprose the same wild wicked jingle of glass,
And chorus on chorus from bellows of brass,
And smoke that went rolling like incense at mass,
Announcing the Captain at 'Evening Class.'

O Stiggins! remember; each Sunday at church
He trolls his loud hymn like a bird on a perch.
He sits by the galley-stove, close to the boys;
He passes the order—'Toe line, and no noise!'
One whisper, one shove, and his natty rattan
Makes naughty boy's cocoa-nut ring like a can;
And last, but not least, when the platter goes round,
Who fumbles so fast in his trousers profound,
And hails—'Purser! lay alongside for a pound?'
Place this in the balance, O Stiggins, and groan,
And wish that our Captain's good works were your own.

At last on Old Tin came a marvellous change;
The boatmen remarked he looked sober and strange
He wandered alone on the shingle and sand,
With hat all a-droop and his chin in his hand.

His telescope into the beach would he dig,
And uselessly point his big stick at a brig!
'Our Captain's beam-ended—got whipped in a squall.'
'Young woman?' guessed one. 'Ay, young woman,'
  said all.
Too well they conjectured the cause of his gloom;
And Luce was the name of this damsel of doom.

     Vol. II.

  'La, child! you're a fool!
  My word but he'll cool
If you treat him again like a boy out of school.
At your time of life, too—clean thirty, come Yule!
    You'd best make your hay,
    My girl, while you may,
And 'ware how you scare a last suitor away.
Come, smile at him, Luce, and console your old aunt:
You've teased her enough!'
      But Luce answered, 'I shan't.
  The man that I wed
  Must come early to bed,
Not roar with a gang of bad boatmen instead:
Hooraying and hooting—like cats on the lead.
  Why, Aunt ('cross the lane
  Words pass pretty plain),
I never undress but I hear what they're sayin',
And Tinderbox he's just the worst of the train.
I take him? I tell you I'd sooner be slain!
No use to be one, when we're better as twain.'

  'When boys,' cried the Aunt,
  'In their cups grow gallant,
No decent young woman should listen aslant.

It's nature, not naughtiness, Luce—though I grant
It's awful the way that they chatter and chant;
But find better man than the Captain you can't.
  To see him—la! Luce,
  You cold little goose!
Flit by of a morning, so dapper and spruce,
And blink at our window; and all of no use!
Give *me* a tight fellow, all whisker and bones;
No jelly-fish boiled—like that wretch Joseph Jones!'

  'Who's Jones?' cried the Niece;
  'Who talks of cold geese?
Come, Aunt, why on earth should you trouble my peace?
I'm sure it's high time for *your* fiddle to cease.
  Pray leave me alone!
  It's pretty well known
The snug little penny Pa' left is my own,
And even at thirty one isn't a crone;
And drat me if ever I marry a drone!
So tell your old Captain to alter his tone:
He's used to blow-ups; and, once more—he be blown!
It's all square between us; I'm cross and he's cranky;
He's asked me to have him—and I've said, "No, thank ye!"'

  Ah me! cruel maid!
  Were bitter words weighed?
One week, and your victim was just like a shade.
He walked to and fro, as if pacing a deck;
To 'Cap'n, how are you?' made answer, 'A WRECK.'
Half-masted, the flag on his grotto of shell
Hung loose and dejected: he muffled his bell;
Adjourned *sine nocte* his evening class,
And laid his marines out for dead on the grass.

In meekness and silence he moved in his woe:
'No music—no! Death on board. Band gone below.
'Poor fellow!' said every one down at St. Mark's;
'This here, to be sure, should cure Luce of her larks.'

  And still, as time wore,
  Worse days than before,
It seemed, for our mariner bold were in store:
His cot was unentered—his home was the shore.
Dream-haunted he wandered adrift when the dawn
Lit out the first trouserless teaser of prawn;
Dream-haunted he wandered when lazy machines
Lay axle-deep anchored, and when by no means
The little white ladies kept under their screens.
Dream-haunted still on through the shingle he pressed,
When arrows of sunlight stood sheaved in the west;
And still, through the star-change and wonder of night,
He followed that vanishing glimpse of delight,
And groaned, 'Carry on, sir! and keep chase in sight!'
No breakfast—no luncheon—no dinner at all,
Made every one feel that his chances were small.

  At last he hove short.
  'This cruising's bad sport;
Don't bring one a cabin's length nearer to port.
Come on, then, I say! Who's afraid of a fort?
Come on, if you're one of the real sea sort!
Got licked in your courting? Well, fire in court!
  There's a pair o' land sharks
  Ashore at St. Mark's;
Two lawyers, I mean, with a boat's crew of clerks;
I'll board 'em at once—have a grand consultation—
Explain that I only want solemnization,
Injunction—compunction—and consummization!

Hurrah, Captain Tin ! pipe to night-class as usual :
Up, flag ! with a broadside for them as would use you ill ! '

There's a sweet little stucco-built Gothic abode,
That coyly shrinks back, as it were, from the road,
With a lawn and a fountain and all that is fair,
And pretty French windows to let in the air,
And a shining brass plate on the gate to declare
The name of this Eden :—

> LA SOURICIÈRE.

Within—'tis no fanciful picture portrayed—
'Mid goldfish and birds and the scent and the shade,
Two cool old philosophers work at their trade :
For this is the garden, and these are the sharks
That eat up the flat-fish of sober St. Mark's.

In blundered the Captain, and let out his ' jaw '
At once to those cool old attorneys-at-law.
What passed is a secret. We never presume
To peep or paul-pry in the calm legal room.
And why the old simpleton went there at all,
Or what he expected would come of his call,
Are questions we simple ones can't overhaul,
  But who's to compose
  His senses, who knows
That when—as he always persisted——' Court rose,'
Tin danced out of doors on the tips of his toes,

His hat in the air,
With—' Blest if a pair,
Afloat or ashore, are alive to compare
With Diddle and Wink of La Souricière!
Ah! Luce little knows how we'll bring it all square.
Well done, Captain Tin!
'Tis your turn to grin :
You *have* had a rare six-and-eightpenny spin!
Now, boarders, away there, and haul the girl in!'
The sharks, don't you see, when they took him in tow,
Had thrown a most relishing quid for his quo.

Vol. III.

Imagine the joy
Of boatman and boy
When heard once again was the well-known 'ahoy!'
How 'lubber!' and 'lout!'
Made people turn out,
Quite pleased, as if tickled like so many trout.
'Hurrah! here's our Captain again,' was the shout :
' Miss Luce, to be sure, has been sent right-about.'
Miss Luce didn't like it, of that there's no doubt;
And sat in her window and set up a pout.

No matter : flag flew.
Marines, good and true,
Formed up on the rampart again for review.
Once more, as before,
With revel and roar,
Was midnight made hideous to people next door.
Once more Captain Tin strutted forth like a lord,
His chin in the air, and ' band playing on board.'

So passed a few days;
And now let us raise
At last the long-looked-for sensational blaze
Which ushers our tale to its ultimate phase,
Like bang and blue-light at the pantomime plays.

One night, while at class—
'Don't see how to pass
This life,' said the Captain, ' on gravel and grass :
I'll grow into quite an unwholesome old ass
For want of seafaring and salt-water sa'ce.
Look here, lads, afloat
In my tight little boat
'Cross Channel this evening I'm thinking I'll tote,
And bring back a log-full of something worth note;
So drink to my luck while I ship my sea-coat.'

'To-night! No—no, Cap'n!' those mariners cried;
'No offing, by George, in a flowing spring-tide,
With rain and a dirty nor'-wester outside.'

'Fair wind as could follow!' the Captain replied :
'With compass and lantern and bottle beside,
I'll fetch Calais harbour and breakfast inside
On vin-ordinairy, my boys, and frog fried!'

Persuasion was vain;
Far out on the main
Those mariners followed, with eyes on the strain,
A lantern that danced in the darkness and rain.
'He's gone! We shall never see Cap'n again!
We ought to ha' nailed him, we did—lubbers all!
No use to give chase when you can't overhaul;
And just like a bird goes that clean little yawl.
Poor fellow! he'll surely turn up in a trawl.'

'Boat adrift!' sang the coast-guard. 'Hands out and secure!
Three miles to the south'ard!'
       'Our Cap'n, for sure!
We told him he'd swamp, and we never spoke truer.'

Away through the glitter of sunrise they went,
For the dirty nor'-wester was over and spent;
Away through the emerald waves riding home,
Slow shedding and trailing their plumage of foam;
Away through the living salt scent of the air,
And boarded their prize with a howl of despair;
For compass and lantern and bottle were there,
But the Captain was gone—O! no need to guess where.

   Let us linger no more
   On a subject so sore:
The shops at St. Mark's were shut, window and door;
And desolate fishermen wailed on the shore,
Or mournfully met, their old friend to deplore.
'Poor fellow!' they found it some slight consolation
To murmur, 'His loss will be felt by the nation.'

   Luce wept at the news.
   'Was it well to refuse?
If I hadn't, he'd never have gone for this cruise,
But been at this moment alive in dry shoes.
His death at my door will be laid at St. Mark's—
My door!'
   But it opened, and in walked the Sharks.

'Dear madam, we venture to call,' said the twain,
'With blended sensations of pleasure and pain.
Our amiable client—the worthy departed—
Adored you through life with a love single-hearted;

And, dead though he lies in the depths of the ocean,
This parchment will speak to his deathless devotion.
With every kind wish that your life may be sunny,
He's left you his cot—and the whole of his money!'

    There! Whilst you digest
    That startling bequest,
Suppose that a twelvemonth at least hath ' secessed,'
And Luce all the time has been petted and pressed
By Aunt to do just what was ' business and best,'
And quietly pass to the Tinderbox nest,
And give *her* the pretty blue bedroom sou'-west.
Suppose that poor Luce in the end acquiesced,—
Conceded the bedroom to Aunty's request,
And then—why, suppose that you read for the rest.

Exquisite fingers are busy with tea—
Filling small china cups, one, two, and three:
One for Miss Luce, and another for Aunt;
One for—guess whom—Joseph Jones the gallant!
Fact, I assure you. Observe with what care
Joseph has parted and polished his hair:
Look at his rings, at his wristbands, his tie;
Notice the delicate leer in his eye;
And judge, as you may, why with bosom aglow
Thrills the respectful yet rapturous Joe.
You'll mark, or I greatly mistake, at a glimpse,
A spirit that soars above muffins and shrimps.

    Now this way, now that,
    With twist and with pat
(I mean roll and butter, of course, and all that),
He plies the two ladies and patters his chat;
You'd think that the end would be bigamy flat.

But no—cunning fellow! Joe knows what he's at,
And strokes the old lady down-hair like a cat;
Aware that, although the right side of the mat,
With Aunty *nolente*—no peg for his hat!

Hark! whose is the footstep that sounds on the walk,
With grave, supernatural, stumpety stalk,
And suddenly puts a full stop to their talk—
Makes Luce whisper 'Listen!' and Aunt echo 'Lawk!'
And Joseph, with countenance changing to chalk,
Behave like a little bird under a hawk?

   'Tis he! 'Tis his hum!
   He's coming—he's come!
Like the ghost of a fiddle and corpse of a drum
In dreadful duet sounds his 'rum-tity-tum!'
Tortured and terrified, started they all—
Their faces felt swarming with spiders a-crawl—
A gust of ill-wind shook the prints on the wall,
And fluttered the curtain about like a pall;
And then, 'mid a general scatter and squall,
Over the green mignonette in the window-box
Peered the mahogany face of Old Tinderbox!

   Luce dropped in a swoon;
   Aunt swallowed her spoon;
Joe's face grew as yellow and moist as the moon;
As togged in blue monkey, with buttons of brass,
Topped with tarpaulin-hat shining like glass,
Telescope tucked *à la fusil de chasse*,
Entered the jolly old Captain.
       'Ho, lass!
What call to go sobbin' and looking aghas'?
Come, wake up again, and go in for a glass!

Ho, ho! So you thought I was down for a drownder?
Not I! Got picked up by a Dutch outward-bounder;
And here I am safe, and I never was sounder!
Been all round the world since I looked in those eyes!'
(O Diddle and Wink, what a cargo of lies!)
' And brighter than ever, my pretty, they shine,
Which, darn my bad luck! is no business of mine.
Wake up, little lady! For fear o' mishaps,
In case, don't you see, that my life might elapse,
I wrote up a paper and left you my traps.

' Well now, I'm too happy at *not* being bunked:
Ay; no one should grumble who isn't defunct:
So keep 'em for ever, and welcome, sweet Luce;
Without you, my precious, those traps are no use!
   Good-bye, blessed pet!
   Don't grizzle and fret:
I'm whalebone all over, and young enough yet—
In fact, every Sunday the younger I get.
I'll shin my own way up the ladder of life again,
And hang me if ever I try for a wife again!'

   ' Ah, Captain!—no, no!
   Indeed you shan't go!'
Cried Luce, with her pretty face all in a glow.
' Here's tea on the table—three cups in a row!
And Aunt has a cupboard of brandy below;
(You've brought your own baccy, I hope, for a blow;)
And Peggy shall devil such *beautiful* bones,
And Jones was just going:—*Good* night, Joseph Jones!'

EMMA AND EGINARD.

A STORY OF CHARLEMAGNE.

'Les traditions attribuent à Eginard l'honneur d'avoir épousé Emma, fille de Charlemagne ; et l'aventure qui amena, dit-on, ce mariage est l'un des souvenirs les plus populaires de notre vieille histoire. Là voici telle que la rapporte la chronique du Monastère de Lauresheim.'—Guizot, *Histoire de la Civilisation en France*, vol. ii. p. 218.

   Ho, butler mine ! the goblet bring,
    And cross the brim with mystic wine !
   Ho, Muses nine ! on airy wing,
    Descend, and weave the fiery line !

Ho, gallant pen ! run merrily, and fling me forth a strain,
Right worthy of the noble theme that warms within my brain,
Of that great King of Christendom, the glorious Charlemagne !

Lord of the frozen Baltic, Lord of the German pines—
Lord of Italian valleys, and mountains thick with vines,
That look on Spanish headlands, where the dying day declines.

A thousand years are past and gone, yet long may poets sing,
What, to the base mechanic ear, much wonder yet may bring,
How the illustrious Charlemagne was ' every inch a King ! '

For eight foot, quite,
Was his Highness' height
As he towered along on his Boulevards bright:
And small people scuttled away in a fright,
Before they got stepped on—like beetles at night;
And his chain- and plate-armour of gold were a sight;—
While, as for his sabre,
'Twould cost you less labour
To 'put' the big stone or go 'tossing the caber,'
Than vainly strive to poise and swing
The terrible blade of the strong old King!
His own right hand,
Alone in the land,
Might wield in the battle that ponderous brand,
Whose ruthless edge,
So legends allege,
Descending with crash like an armourer's sledge,
Could cleave a stout foeman of infidel breed
Through turban and breastplate, hip, saddle and steed,
A cut, as his aides-de-camp all were agreed,
The shortest by far for confuting his creed.
And, if cracking the poll
Seems rather droll,
By way of a tonic dispensed for the soul,
Charlemagne didn't see it, and couldn't control
His zeal for the Church when him listed unroll
Her orthodox flag,
Delighting to brag
Of multiplied converts brought safely to bag:
Of Saxon and Saracen
Marched up to Paris, on
Purpose to have them baptized by the garrison,
Or churched in a way that was quick by comparison:

'Till superfine saints looked immensely mysterious,
And the clergy pronounced him ' decidedly serious.'

   Yet, woe to the great!
   Since envy and fate
Are always combining to libel their state.
Charlemagne, it is written in all of his lives,
Had a sadly Salt-lakish assortment of wives.
   Some think three or four;
   Some hint at a score:
I wrote in my haste—' a respectable *corps*,'
But the adjective's wrong, which of course we deplore.
   So, seeing in fact
   One can't be exact,
Our muse has discovered a sad want of tact,
By placing us all in a painful dilemma
To choose a mamma for the beautiful Emma.

No matter! such scandal we ought to forget.
Why cloud the name of the sweet brunette?
   Enough to know
   That, years ago,
A thousand at least—but chronology's low—
The exquisite eyes of the princess, our heroine,
Each gentleman's breast had at least put one arrow in.
   As well they might,
   For a pair so bright,
Set off with so charming a figure and height,
Don't flash every day, which is lucky and right,
Or ' crowners' might ' quest it' from morning to night.
And, e'en in those days—for my tale, you're aware,
Dates back to the time when all maidens were fair,
And enchanted princesses weren't anyway rare;
Even then, there was not, on the world-wide horizon,
A star like our Emma whom all set their eyes on!

Swaggering captains, cased in plate,
Snorted sighs through helmet-grate :
She liked them well—but bade them wait.

Velvet courtiers, trim and neat,
Poured their sorrows at her feet :
She liked them too—they smelt so sweet.

Sovereign princes fared no better :
None could link the golden fetter :
She only ' wished that they might get her.'

Cynosures resent all pressure :
Man must wait their pretty pleasure :
Worship till their golden leisure.

Now the fiery Charlemagne
I need scarcely explain,
After all that I've said, had a noble disdain
Of every accomplishment idle and vain ;
And loved to declare
That a jewel so rare
Deserved to be set with unusual care,
For some brother-monarch to win and to wear !

Said he, ' With your boarding-school simper and starch
  I cannot and will not away ;
My daughter shall trip it in Intellect's march,
  A trifle ahead of her day.
Her dawning mind shall not be filled
  By any bleak old woman ;
I'll have her drilled, by a tutor skilled,
  In learning quite uncommon.

Logic and Latin, and Greek, may be,
  Shall my own young chaplain teach her;
For he is a scholar of strange degree,
  And withal a wonderful preacher.
He reads by night, and he reads by day,
  Both Gradus and Delectus;
And she shall learn more, ere her years be a score,
  Than you'd put in a short prospectus.
So train her and teach her, my chaplain true,
  Much learning grave and stately;
For I were full fain that her scholarly strain
  Should make men marvel greatly!'

  Ho, chivalrous Macaulay!
    A boon, my liege, I claim:
  You've puzzled us so sorely,
    You can't refuse the same.
  Ho! did our fathers bully
    Their chaplains with such glee,
  As you paint, so very coolly,
    In your famous Chapter III?
  Did each man keep a curate
    For his own especial snubbing,
  At such a very poor rate
    As a ten-pound note, with grub in?
      To fetch and to carry,
      And trundle a barry,
      And never to marry,
      And live in a garret
      On cow-beef and carrot,
Nail up the plums and say grace like a parrot,
    And dub him 'Young Levite?'
  Stuff! who's to believe it?
Our 'Quarterly' heretics will not receive it.

They swear you've perverted
What Eachard asserted,
And cunningly told 'em
What isn't in Oldham ;
So, as for the scales, I'd be sorry to hold 'em.
I've only to say
That, in Charlemagne's day,
Good people knew better, and loved to display
Their zeal for the Church in a liberal way,
And blew out their chaplains with punch and tokay,
And crammed them with turtle and doubled their pay,
Delighted to see them both portly and gay.
But, pray don't suppose
That here I propose
To paint a great priest with a glorified nose,
And a corpulent belly, and corns on his toes !
No ! Out on the bard
Who could ever be hard
On that model pet-parson—the dear Eginard !

O, tea-tables of Cheltenham !—
O, spinster Saints of Bath !
What interest you'd have felt in him,
How thronged his primrose path !
For his words were O so silky,
And his doctrine O so milky,
And never in a shrill key
Did he shriek out horrid things !
But so blandly he'd entreat you,
So benignly half-way meet you,
That really in his seat you
Saw an angel without wings.

They say, 'a little learning
   Is a dangerous sort of thing;'
Which useful hint returning,
The Muse begs leave to sing,
That a very little tutoring
   May work a man more woe,
Than all the downright suitoring
   He'll ever undergo.
If you doubt it or deny it,
   Choose a cousin bright and young;
For a fortnight fairly try it;
   Teach her some outlandish tongue—
Teach her conics—teach her magic—
   Teach her anything you know,
'Till you find your tone grow tragic,
   And your bosom toss and glow;
'Till you groan out ghastly adjec-
     tives in whispers hoarse and low.
'Till your friends crack jokes ironic,
   And you feel a weary wish
For a whiff of gas carbonic,
   Cooked in a charcoal dish:
'Till in short you learn how lightly
   Is the human heart divine
Fenced against eyes that brightly,
   Alas, too brightly, shine!
So shall you feel due sympathy
   For our reverend young beau,
If, mazed in Cupid's dim path, he
   Shall chance at last on woe.
But, how he fared with Emma's eyes,
   We leave to Part the Second;
Wherein his cast of blank or prize
   Shall all be duly reckoned.

PART THE SECOND.

Dear Alma Mater! as in duty bound,
    I love thy gray old walls. I love to tread
Thy voiceless cloisters, and to hear the sound
    Of my slow footfall echo overhead.
I love the sacred stream that floats around
    Those palaces of the immortal dead.
We spoke of mathematics, and I am
At once—in heart at least—beside the Cam.

To me, its idle ooze recalls a time
    When one looked out so bravely on the world:
When hearts were free to fight, and hands to climb
    Its difficult heights, and thence to fling unfurled
The banner of their thought—that young sublime!
    Alas, how tamely in a nutshell curled,
Sleeps all its fiery promise! Yes—of late,
Enthusiasm's clearly out of date.

We hoard it for some cyclical 'Aggression,'
    Or grand new cosmopolitan Bazaar;
Perhaps its force increases by compression—
    And now, I really wonder where we are?
The man who can unravel this digression,
    And tell me how I ever strayed so far
From aught and all in Part the First recorded,
Shall find himself most handsomely rewarded.

        Well!—to proceed—
        Never, indeed,
Was a royal phenomenon trained with such speed;

For, long ere the sweet little princess was twenty,
She'd carol off slick the whole *As in præsenti*,
Had a competent knowledge of *Propria quæ
Maribus*, and much learning of lesser degree :
So kindly, in short, did she take to her tutor
She'd really no time to encourage a suitor.

   Now it seems that the day,
    Between teaching and play,
Imperceptibly glided so quickly away,
That our excellent Mentor was forced to propose
To borrow a slice from the hours of repose.
   And as teaching by night,
   By the merry lamp light,
In a lady's boudoir isn't orthodox quite,
And as Emma's apartment, so fragrant and gay,
Lay across the court-yard—in short, over the way,
Involving some nice points of ingress and egress, he
Thought it high time for a choice bit of secrecy.
   So, pointing out clearly
   The day wasn't nearly
So useful—if only for star-gazing, merely—
He went on to hint that, as folks might be shocked
If he chanced to stay late, and in consequence knocked
People up when the castle was all doubled-locked,
   He meant to crawl out
   Of his window :—no doubt
He should very well find his way down by the spout ;
And, if she'd let him in, why, there wasn't a doubt
Her progress in Science would amply repay
For an ocean of obstacles braved by the way !

'O shocking imprudence !' I hear you exclaim,
' How could she—how dare she ? O ! fie and for shame !

How can Mr. Bentley permit you to edit
Such scandal?'
    I only assert that I read it
In Lauresheim's Annals,—they're quoted by Guizot,[1]
Whose note on the subject at once will appease you.

  Heavily swayed the midnight bell,
  Counting slow its ponderous knell:
  Where through the lattice a taper had shone,
  Lattice was open and taper was gone.
    For the slim Eginard
    Hath tied a knot hard
In his reverend garters—the lattice unbarred,
    And, like Leotard,
    Spun into the yard;
    And crawling and creeping,
    And craftily peeping,
This way and that, though good people were sleeping
    Warm in their beds,
    Nor troubling their heads
For a lively chaplain over the leads,
    He gains the boudoir,
    Taps at the door,
And—there let us leave him, till day-break once more
Dawns gray through the darkness on turret and shore.

  Merrily chimed the matin bell,
    At six o'clock in the morning:
  It broke up a loving and learned spell,
    With its unmistakable warning.
  The tutor so grave and the pupil so shy
  Just peeped out once with inquisitive eye,
  As people will do before wishing 'good-bye,'

[1] Histoire de la Civilisation en France, ii. 219.

As a hint that it's time to be going;
When poor Eginard, with a dismal cry,
Shrieked—'Here's a kettle of fish to fry!
Now, Saints protect us! out of the sky
I'm shot if it hasn't been snowing!
The ground's as white as white can be!
They'll track my steps!—it's up to your knee!
They'll hunt me home—those villanous men—
They'll put out my eyes, with an inky pen,
And throttle me dead in my peaceful den!
  Saints on high,
  Look down and try
If you couldn't for once let a gentleman fly?
A pair of wings and a tail to match
Across the yard—and never a batch
Of candles blazed on an altar yet
Like those for which I'll be in your debt!'

  But never a word
  From Saint he heard;
It was clear that they thought it extremely absurd
Of a good beast to make an indifferent bird.
He felt before, and he felt behind,
But nothing unusual there could he find.
The startled princess wished him flown;
It was very unpleasant to hear him groan:
At last she thought of a plan of her own.
'Listen to me, my tutor dear,'
Said she—'there's really nothing to fear.
  One thing's clear,
  You can't stay here
'Till the beak and the feathers you talk of appear.
Why, you mightn't be fledged by the end of the year!

Jump on my shoulders :—it's not very far :
I'll carry you over ; and—there you are !
My tiny print will scarcely break
The carpet of the crisping flake ;
And if, perchance, my track be known,
Say that *Sonnambula walked alone !*
Scandal's self must own that here
Your innocence, at least, is clear.
Eginard—Eginard ! do let me try :
It's no use your flapping : you never can fly.'

    Small was the need
    For the lady to plead,
For the chaplain was very much frightened indeed,
And jumped on her back with incredible speed ;
    Begged her to trot;
    Cried that his lot
Was a great deal too hard—he'd be lynched on the spot !
Come ! couldn't she canter ?—it wasn't so hot !

The poor little princess was doing her best ;
She stumbled on, with a panting breast.
Stoutly and safely she carried him through,
'Till he clutched the string of his garters true ;
Then kindly watched him up the spout,
Shinning and spinning in ether and doubt ;
Stopping half-way for a sprawl and a shout,
And yelling to know what the Saints were about ;
And so she watched and watched, until
She watched him over the window-sill.
Then, flushed and breathless, homeward fled
The sweet princess, and only said
' To judge by the way my dear tutor takes wing,
Learning is doubtless a dangerous thing ! '

PART THE THIRD.

Charlemagne sat in his window,
    A-drinking early-purl;
Twelve barbers stood behind him,
    The royal wig to curl.
Twelve Paladins were kneeling
    Around him in a ring;
Twelve trumpeters were pealing
    At once, 'God save the King!'
Twelve courtiers took their places,
    The royal jokes to praise;
To hand the royal braces,
    Or lace the royal stays.

All of a sudden he starts from his chair;
The very wig-royal flew straight in the air,
As he staggered and shouted:—'Good gracious! look there!
Look, gentlemen, LOOK!'
                        If the Limited Mail
Had snipped off the tip of Beelzebub's tail,
While quietly drunk and asleep on the rail,
    Not Nick the Satanic,
    In pain and in panic,
Had bounced up with symptoms so loud and galvanic,
Or hurled such a broadside at stoker and guard,
As the furious Charlemagne at our poor Eginard!
And, indeed, though a moralist, captious and slow,
Might have fancied his expletives rather *de trop*,
And prayed him, in nautical language, to 'stow'
Some pithy imperatives, such a tableau
As a talented daughter, full trot through the snow,

With, perched on her shoulder, a dandy young beau,
Was, rather, what Cockneys describe as 'a go!'

   Bluer than blue
   The courtiers grew;
They didn't know what upon earth to do.
   If pulling long faces
   With frightful grimaces
Were anyway useful towards keeping their places,
Theirs were at least on a durable basis;
For they thumped their breasts and rolled their eyes,
And filled the hall with their dismal cries.
   Nay, one was seen,
   His shrieks between,
Indulging in anguish more dreadly serene;
For he buried his face in the tail of his coat,
And stuffed his handkerchief down his throat!

   Thundered the King:—
   'Ho, gentlemen, bring
That insolent boy from a beam to swing!
   Turn out the guard
   In the great court-yard!
Breakfast be hanged!—till we've hanged Eginard!'

   Charlemagne sat in his window,
    Still drinking early-purl;
   His daughter stood before him,
    Her hair was out of curl.
Her downcast eyes were counting
    The tangled carpet-rushes;
The royal blood ran mounting
    Through her cheeks in crimson blushes.
I would you had witnessed his Majesty's grin,
As they dragged the terrified chaplain in;

His glowering scowl,
As he said with a growl,
'Good youth, can't you see that it's useless to howl?
How think you, my lords, shall we hang him or stick him?
Or, first of all set a strong fellow to lick him?
How would your wisdoms advise us to slaughter
The rascal that dares to make love to our daughter?'

  Then the spiteful courtiers gladly
   Suggested sundry ways;
  All which would hurt him sadly,
   And bequeath to future days
  Sermons for those who madly
   On a princess dared to gaze!
They talked of needles—they talked of pins;
Of singeing his whiskers, and scraping his shins;
  Of a rack to crack
  The small of his back;
Of drowning him slowly, done up in a sack;
Of toasting him gently—of boiling him hard;
Of a jolly Guy Fawkes in the tournament-yard;
In short, how to pickle our poor Eginard,
With anything like a respectful regard
  To his Majesty's taste,
  Which was cruelly chaste,
Was a problem they couldn't resolve in such haste.
They couldn't decide if a boil or a roast
Would turn, in a way that would worry him most,
A nice young curate into a ghost!

  Perchance you've watched a hungry bear
   Snarling over a bone;
  If so, you may picture his Majesty's glare,
   And fancy his Majesty's tone!

For in thunder rolled his anger,
    And the courtiers held their breath;
Emma thought he meant to hang her,
    And she stood as white as death.
And her lover grew so funky,
    He couldn't stand at all;
But, like a poisoned monkey,
    Rolled gibbering round the hall.

    'Daughter mine,
    You've taken the shine
Out of our highly respectable line!
You have: you've disgraced us! I'm cruelly hurt.
How could you—how durst you—you baggage, go flirt
With a beggar? he's scarcely a tail to his shirt!
Don't answer:—I see you intend to be pert.
The shame and the scandal 'twould only make worse,
Or I'd send you together to church—in a hearse.
Now hear me, and heed me. We won't, in our ire,
Roll from the frying-pan into the fire;
We must act as a King, though we feel as a Sire.
We pardon our daughter—for reasons of state:
Towards our chaplain, we bid the wrath-royal abate:
Our courtiers we rather advise to relate
    What they've seen of their tricks,
    If they're anxious to 'fix'
A precious long mile t'other side of the Styx,
Where Paris ain't half as well known as old Nick's:
And finally, girl, since you've chosen to carry him,
We stand no more nonsense. My child, you must marry him!'

    Then smiling spoke the courtiers,
    That stood before the King:—

'Though we talked of fire and tortures,
   We knew they weren't the thing.
We knew your Royal Highness,
   And we knew your bosom ran
With the cream of human kindness
   For this excellent young man.
And we only spoke in joking—
   So please you, gracious King—
When we said we'd set him croaking,
   Or any such-like thing.
May our chaplain wax and flourish!
   May he wear the Scarlet Hat!
May the princess yearly nourish
   A churchling fair and fat!
May it ever be a lesson t' her,
   This blessed morning's fun!
Now, how could we speak pleasanter,
   O Magne! than we have done?
And if any of us mention
   Her charming little whim,
Or breathe a reprehension
   By inuendo dim,
Sire! strike him off his pension,
   And strike his head off him!'

THE CONJUROR'S CALL.

A LOG behind the roaring bars—
  Before them sat John Horn,
As long and strong and red as Mars—
  A burly man of corn.

He filled another tankard-full,
  And fired another pipe:
The north-wind bellowed like a bull
  Clutched in a lion's gripe.

The snow-storm, all about the grange,
  Beat fiercely in the dark.
'Blow on—snow on! Don't chop and change!'
  John's voice was like a bark.

'Blow on—snow on, in squall and gust!
  Thunder, and frighten Jane!
Mine has been usage of the worst
  That ever gave man pain.

'Blow on—snow on! She can't forget
  The times we've been together.
Smite on, with raging wind and wet,
  Disastrous winter-weather!

THE CONJUROR'S CALL.

' Tumble that barn and pigeon-loft—
   Blast all those trees a-growing!
And blow her into something soft,
   And then—give over blowing!'

So spake John Horn in fume and wrath,
   Accosting winds unruly;
And then he blew his tankard-froth,
   And whiffed away more coolly.

   A tap upon the pane,
      A rattling at the door—
John Horn undid the chain,
      And in came wind and roar;
   And one all battered and white,
      Stamping out of the storm :
' Farmer, an ugly night!
   Stand us a bit of a warm.
This man's lost in valley and wold,
And it is bitterly, beastly cold!'

' Come in!' said the great red host :
   ' Sit down, and toast your shins.
World's all white as a ghost,
   Wind's like needles and pins.

' Yonder's a pipe and a jug,
   Also a homebake and bacon ;
Then make a bed o' the rug ;
   A better one never was shaken.

' My stars! what a comical hat!
   Odds bobs, but you've found the mad hatter!
And why's your coat made of a mat—
   Or else what's it got that's the matter?

' And what makes you blink like a cat,
    And stuff your great toes in the fire ?
I'm darned if I know what you're at—
    And that's just the short of it, squire !'

' This is a Conjuror, John Horn,'
    That weird old man did say;
' He cannot wait for morrow-morn ;
    He must be leagues away.
Ninety-and-nine he hath to go,
Ere you shall hear your Dorkings crow.

' His hat that, in irreverent tone,
    You talk about as comical,
Moulded upon a load-stone cone,
    Is absolutely conical.

' His coat was once a famous fit,
    For flame or frost adjustable.
His toes, I s'pose, are gone to grit ;
    You see they're incombustible.

' Come, wake up straight, and poke the grate !
    He's beastly cold, Horn John !
He's lame and old, and out of gait—
    But, on—he must jog on !'

John rubbed and mentioned both his eyes :
    ' I tell you what, my hearty,—
The Rule-o'-Three's a fool,' says he,
    ' To you—you old Third party.

'But if you're bound, my boy, to march
   Through all this blow and snow,
I'll brew you something that'll starch
   Your backbone as you go!'

His great match-tankard John brought out,
   And, with a jovial hum,
He mixed and gaily stirred about
   The lemon, loaf, and rum.

'Now, Crinky-cranky! take your pull,'
   He cried, and passed the flagon;
''Twill make you frisky as a bull,
   And fit to haul a waggon!'

The silver bowl the Conjuror took,
   And opened his mouth wide,
And poured it, like a boiling brook,
   Straight into his inside.

'Hurrah, John Horn! you jolly dog!
   Here's ten ton off this back.
Was ever such a pound of grog!
   Shake hands. How are you, Jack?

'He's going—going. Almost gone.
   Your door will soon be shut on him.
Now: will you put his hat on, John,
   And stand him up and button him?

'That's nicely; thank you. Off he goes.
   He'll see his way pre-sently.
Perhaps, John, you could point his nose,
   And push him—rather gently.

'O bless him, stop! John, ha'n't you got
  Some wish that wants fulfilling?
Out with it, John, upon the spot:
  You'll find this Conjuror willing.

'He don't forget he's in your debt
  For kindness most particular.
Now, don't you start him, John, just yet;
  But hold him perpendicular.'

John winced, and grinned a sheepish grin,
  And blushed like any butcher.
'My sweetheart's bin and took me in—
  I mean, won't let me touch her.

'If you could set us fair and square;
  And start us once more courtin',
I'm blessed,' said John, with liberal air,
  'If I don't make your fortun'!'

'He'll see to all you mention, John.
  'Fore long that girl you'll dandle.
He's glad you're walking same way, John—
  'Cause you can car' the candle.

'These canny folk can put a spoke
  In other people's wheels;
Though round the world they poke and croak,
  Themselves with empty creels.

'Now, John, one little tiny nudge,
  And off we go, together'—
And off the Conjuror went a-trudge,
  Alone in the wild weather.

John heard his cries all over the wold:
'Isn't it bitterly, beastly cold?'

At break of morn strode forth John Horn,
    Amid a world of snow:
He walked about his farm forlorn;
    He heard his Dorkings crow.

Of sheep and kine, and ducks and swine,
    Came gloomy revelations:
Last night had taken all the shine
    Off several calculations.

He walked as one who doubts and dreams,
    In puzzle and in pain;
'Till, down among the frozen streams,
    He suddenly met Jane!

She didn't speak—she didn't stir—
    All in white satin sneezing—
While Fahrenheit's thermometer
    Stood inches under 'freezing.'

'Good gracious, Jane! what freak insane
    Has brought you from your mother's?
I've nine pigs nipped in yonder lane,
    And you'll be like the others!

'Your eyes are pink—your cheeks are blue—
    You aren't in proper clothes:
You've got the influenza, too—
    And a raspberry on your nose!'

Jane's face was crisping far too fast
   For either pout or simper;
But fluttered from her lips at last
   A little chilly whimper:

'Dear John,' she said, 'I've been quite wrong
To keep you waiting this ever-so-long.
Come! wrap me quick in your cloak's great fold:
It is so bitterly, beastly cold!'

THE ROSE OF BASSORA.

A BALLAD OF TRUE LOVE.

'My love is like the red, red rose.'—Old Song.

A LONG time ago lived a wealthy Bashaw,
   Who ruled the fine town of Bassora ;
His word as a matter of course was the law,
   His beautiful daughter's name—Laura.

Her figure was fine, and her face was divine,
   In profile the rarest Circassian :
While her fingers and feet were so cruelly neat,
   They'd have stirred a brass monkey to passion.

Now a prince to provide for so dainty a bride
   Was the one thing that puzzled his life out ;
If a suitor applied who offended his pride,
   Pa' stood on the mat, with his knife out.

' Look here, Sir ! ' he'd say—' if you don't march away
   This moment—here goes at your vitals !
A man must bring tin, my daughter to win,
   With at least his half-hundred of titles ! '

Is it needful to tell that this brilliant young belle
   Had her own little notions, in private?
That *her* mind had been clear, on one point, for a year,
   Just the point Papa couldn't arrive at?

Of course not. The fact is, she'd long put in practice
   A sadly undutiful scheme,
With a handsome young Persian—her father's aversion,
   Who wrote *billets-doux* by the ream.

Like a 'Bul-bul' he sang—O such soft, creamy slang;
   (Don't blast the nice bird in a fury!)
Like a Dervish he danced, as he gaily advanced,
   To 'turn' some electrified houri.

From bright Ispahan came this gifted young man,
   A Sheik, rather highly connected;
Stay, I *can* cram his name in—'twas Iky-ben-jāmen,
   Universally loved and respected.

When the stars on the river were all in a quiver,
   A little canoe would drop down
To a certain snug bower, and wait there an hour,
   Then shoot away back to the town.

I know not, alas, how the thing came to pass—
   Some people suspicions *will* harbour;
But one cloudy night, with his eyes very bright,
   PAPA sat alone in the arbour.

Down glided the boat—'She's there!' from afloat
   Came the whisper:—'My rose of Bassora!
Good lord! what a squeeze! oh, gently love, please!
   Let GO my nose! O, I say! LAURA!'

How quick the transition from transports Elysian!
  The angry Bashaw was quite brutal.
Ten slaves, at his beck, took the Sheik by the neck,
  'Till resistance was perfectly futile.

'In our Dungeons of Doom give this puppy-dog room!
  To-morrow let headsman and gibbet
Stand ready by noon, when he'll try a new tune,
  And a dance upon daylight exhibit.'

So swore the Bashaw, by his Prophet and Law,
  In tones which were perfectly frightful;
And nobody doubted the Sheik would be knouted,
  And hung the next day before nightfall.

Next morning, however, his vizier so clever
  Said, 'Pray, Sir, think twice ere you do it.
His friends are of might, and they're safe to show fight;—
  Your Highness may probably rue it.'

Bashaw replied, 'Stuff! He shall die dead enough;
  I've not only said but I've sworn it.
Would you have me, man, break my oath that's at stake,
  To pardon this cursed young hornet?'

'Indeed, Sir, not I. You have sworn he shall die:
  Let's *dye* him as black as a crow, Sir!
Your oath will keep sound, and your child, I'll be bound,
  Won't fancy so smutty a beau, Sir!'

Replied the old bear, 'Ay, the joke will be rare!
  At once to our tan-pits escort him:
Pitch him souse in the vat—make him black as my hat.
  For once, we postpone the *post mortem.*'

One long wretched week, our unfortunate Sheik,
  In lather and agony toiling,
His flesh-brushes plied, scrubbing holes in his hide,
  And went through a mild course of boiling.

Each advertised soap was a new gleam of hope ;
  He tried Mr. Rowland's Kalȳdor ;—
(I hope the *y*'s long—beg pardon if wrong,)
  And the cruel result almost cried o'er :

For blooming red streaks, upon ebony cheeks
  Stole forth in quite floral profusion ;
One's impulse, no doubt, would have been to cry out,
  'Uncle Tom, you old rogue ! you've been rouging !'

In fact, all was vain :—not one inch of the stain
  Gave way before foul means or fair.
To a man with a headful of love this was dreadful ;
  Ben-jāmen gave way to despair.

And, pining away, he grew thinner each day ;
  Sighing, 'Ah, shall I ever persuade her—
That exquisite Laura—to see an adorer
  In the form of a Black Serenader ?'

O, woman !—hem,—*ladies !* (beg pardon),—how great is
  Your sex's unshrinking devotion !
I've thrown down my pen, (picking up same again,)
  In a fit of the wildest emotion.

There ! thank you,—'tis over ! now Muse, little rover,
  Come back to your sober vocation ;
And state what occurred, when our heroine heard
  Of her Iky's transmogrification.

They told her the tale, and silent and pale
   She listened. 'Poor father!' she muttered;
'The older you grow, the less do you know
   On which side your breakfast is buttered.

'Of lovers professed, Iky loves me the best;
   I don't care how dingy his hues are!
Your wit in displaying, you'll find you've been playing
   A game that's adapted for two, Sir!

'He sha'n't think I scorn him, and write a forlorn hymn,
   Sad-headed, 'The negro's petition!'
No! If I can't bleach him, at least I can teach him
   How little *I* care for derision.'

To her chamber she paced, and coolly unlaced
   Her frock, and her stays,—if she wore 'em;
A snowy chemise came next,—oh, now, please!
   My dear ma'am, don't murmur, 'decorum!'

I'm really not going to turn out too knowing—
   No cause for alarm on that head, ma'am;—
You need simply suppose she took off all the clothes
   Which *you* wouldn't carry to bed, ma'am.

And then from a drawer in her gilt escritoire,
   Not laudanum—as perhaps you expected,
But a phial of ink—'twas 'INDELIBLE PINK
   FOR MARKING,' she calmly selected.

And oh, such a sin! o'er her exquisite skin,
   Neck, bosom, feet, fingers and face, ma'am,
Behind and before, she rubbed in rather more
   Than a lifetime was like to erase, ma'am.

There! now the deed's done, and she sits in the sun,
    (Sun shines very warm at Bassora,)
'Till her glossy skin dries, and she looks, bless her eyes!
    Like a sealing-wax model of Laura.

Then she dressed and she ran to her father's divan,
    Upsetting his brandy-and-water;
'See, father!' she cried, 'my lover you've dyed,
    And I've done as much for your daughter!'

Just fancy the row! The Bashaw cried, 'I vow,
    You're too bad,—'pon my soul, you are, Laura!
This cursed connexion—that ruined complexion,—
    Confound you, girl, this *is* a floorer!

'No matter:—begone! I'm a fool to take on
    Like this,—go! get out of my sight, Miss!
You'll play *rouge et noir* with your father no more:
    Bah! marry black Iky to-night, Miss!'

There! more if you'd learn, I'd advise you to turn
    To any 'third volume' that's handy;
And mark how Misfortune strikes work Hymen's porch in,
    And every one eats sugar-candy.

It will save common-places—Pa's horrid fierce faces,
    All sympathy sternly repressing;
The fond couple kneeling—the fine burst of feeling,
    And pardon—turned up with a blessing!

And they lived, O so long, and they loved, O so strong,
   And their features grew daily less shady;
'Till the Sheik merely looked like a very dark man,
   And his wife like a very warm lady.

And if ever you ride by the Tigris so wide,
   A tourist or learned explorer,
You'll hear the tale told of Ben-jāmen the Bold,
   And his blooming Red Rose of Bassora!

ERMENGARDE.

A LEGEND OF THE RHINE.

[*Translated from an ancient Manuscript, lately discovered in the University Library at Bonn.*]

'Verily,' answered Don Quixote, 'you have told one of the rarest tales, fables, or histories imaginable; and your way of telling and concluding it is such as never was, nor will be, seen in one's whole life!'—*Don Quixote*, b. iii. c. 5.

PART I.

THE thunders of the Great Crusade
   Resound along the Rhine;
With angry light of lance and blade
   Her hundred castles shine.
The war-bells, hot with swinging,
   Clash in each fretted spire;
On the dusk mountain springing,
   Red leaps the nightly fire!
The gallant vassals muster,
   To their feudal standards true;
With a slight amount of bluster
   As to what they mean to do:
For the pricking of a dirk
Through the middle of a Turk,

The Pope and all his cardinals had voted a 'good work'
That all the ten commandments entitled one to shirk,
For goodness knows how many years—I shouldn't like to
    state 'em ;
Which, on the Rhine, was held, it seems, no small *desideratum ;*
And, if you slew a couple, as they proved by calculation,
The killing of the last would count in supererogation !
So gladly rushed the clansmen from the ploughshare and
    the vine,
To follow their stern chieftains through the sands of Palestine !

    Beneath old Rheineck's bristling gate
        The fiery gallants throng,
    And curse the fate that bids them wait ;
        For their chieftain tarries long.
The spearsmen are growing excessively drunk,
And bawling their battle-cry, ' Who's in a funk !'
The horsemen are belted and eager to mount ;
Where is their master, the shaggy old Count ?

    The Count, all clad in clanking mail,
        Still strides his warrior hall ;
    His brows are knit and his lips are pale,
    Though nobody yet knew him ever to fail
        At the trumpet's brazen call.
    But he is as jealous as jealous can be,
    For the bride of his bosom is fair to see ;
        And it frets him sore
        To be off to the war,
And leave her unguarded a twelvemonth or more ;
And he's racking his brains for a feasible plan
For guarding her well from a fancy-man !

Meanwhile the sweet young Ermengarde
    Sat in her chamber crying,
She heard the trampling in the yard—
    She saw the standards flying.

She thought of moonlight battle-plains,
    Where wounded men lay screaming,
With long pink slits in all their veins,
    Warm blood-pools round them steaming!

And 'Oh,' cried she, 'this poor old soul,
    To me so very kind,
That on to his steed can scarcely roll
    When two men hoist behind,
How shall he stand the charging line?
    How mad of him to go!
To find a grave in Palestine,
    And eave me weeds and woe!
I had no choice in choosing him—
    They say he's fifty-three;
But still the thought of losing him
    Is very sad to me;
Though I might have married better,
    So I've heard my mother say,
But my father was his debtor,
    And with me he chose to pay!

'But, hark! he comes—once more to claim
My prayers, and say that he's always the same!
I know 'tis he, for nobody swears
Like the dear old Count in getting up stairs!'

    The Count strode in,
      With a tender grin,
    To grunt his last adieu;

And, foolish old man!
Full of a plan
For keeping a pretty wife true!
He hummed and hawed, and stroked his chin,
For he didn't see well at which end to begin;
Then said, 'Ermengarde,
It's bitterly hard
That I should ride off to be pummelled and scarred,
Where much may occur my return to retard,
Such as getting tucked up in a strange churchyard,
With my pockets picked and my brain-pan starred;
And I leave you, my dear,
In horrible fear
Of strange young gentlemen visiting here;
Recollect, you're not out of your teens by a year.
I know, Ermengarde, you're extremely discreet;
But, before I set off, I must beg and entreat
You'll never so much as *look* into the street;
That you'll live like a mouse
At the top of the house,
And simply exert all your feminine *nous*
On the maids and the darning—and always, at night,
Send some one to ask if the gates are all right,
And they're perfectly sure the portcullis is tight,
And the drawbridge is up, and the lanterns alight!
And, one thing more, pray wear this ring;
I know 'tis an old-fashioned, rum-looking thing,
But, let me tell you, that ring was made
Of a crucifix worn in the first Crusade;
And pray observe,
If ever you swerve
From your duty to me in the tiniest curve,
That wonderful ring
Will at once take wing,

To me, as its master, a message to bring!
What a comfort for you—to be sure, that I know
You're perfectly faithful, wherever I go!'

   ' You may tell me 'tis hard,'
   Said the sweet Ermengarde,
' That you should ride off to be pummelled and scarred ;
   I can tell you, I feel
   It is worse, a great deal,
To be doubted in this way! and then to appeal
To a sixpenny hoop, that's as big as a wheel!
I didn't expect it! I couldn't have guessed
That doubts of *my* virtue would trouble your breast!
I wonder you dare, sir! to dream of such stuff,
Or tell me that ONE ring isn't enough!
No matter, I'll wear it! I'm dreadfully vexed ;
But the ring you shall have when I welcome you next.
Go, Sir, go! and, if need there be,
Lock up your castle and carry the key!'

  So the Count rode off to Palestine,
   Loud laughing in his sleeve :
  ' O, long in this brass ring of mine
   May Ermengarde believe!'

  Next morning down the trembling Rhine
   The fresh south-wind was blowing,
  As, all beneath the sweet sunshine,
   Young Ermengarde sat sewing.
  And, ' Oh,' she said, ' this hateful ring!—
   I can't get on at all ;
  Each needle *will* that finger sting—
   That finger far too small!

I needn't wear it, surely,
　　　To plague me all day long;
　　Locked in too, so securely,
　　　How could a girl go wrong?
O dear, that I into the river might fling
This horrible, old-fashioned, sixpenny ring!
　　　'Tis too bad, I declare,
　　　　To ask me to wear
Such a trumpery bauble! Why couldn't he spare
A pretty gold locket, with some of his hair?
And I can't, and I won't! so the wretch may lie there,
And fly and tell tales of poor me, if he dare!'
So the ring was shaken with right good will,
And laid in disgrace on the window-sill.

Now I never yet read, whether story or song,
　One single romance of the Rhine,
But the Devil was sure to come out pretty strong
　In his own particular line:
Now sacking a convent, now bagging a soul,
Now swindling a bishop of mitre and stole,
And always contriving to render his rôle
So excessively pleasant, and lively and droll,
People really were pleased when he came to take toll!
　　　　So it's easy to see,
　　　　　None other than he
Could have filled the Count's brain with his fiddle-de-dee
About poor Ermengarde, who's as good as can be;
And nobody else would have ventured to string
Such a cock-and-bull tale on a sixpenny ring;
And nobody else would have dreamt of a trick
Like that in these presents recorded, but Nick.
For, just as the nice little finger was free,
And the needle was going as brisk as a bee,

A shocking black raven came down with a swoop,
And was off to the woods with the luckless hoop!

      A raven—a fright!
      Its eyes were alight
With a horrid red glow, and its tail wasn't tight,
And its beak was all wrong, and its feathers weren't right,
And its croak was obscene, and it smelt of the night,
And it screeched, as it flew, with a fiendish delight!

Poor girl! just imagine her awful surprise!
How she screamed, how she opened her beautiful eyes,
On perceiving the ring was *en route* for the skies!
      But scream high or scream low,
      All's one to a crow;
And away the bird whirred, like a bolt from a bow,
Leaving Ermengarde perfectly stunned by the blow.

      'O dear—O dear!' she sadly sobbed,
       'Was ever wife so vexed?
    First I'm suspected, then I'm robbed:
      I wonder what comes next!
    How *shall* I make the Count believe
      About this horrid bird?
He'll say, 'My dear, you can't deceive
      Men of my age. Absurd!
    Such nursery myths are out of date;
      When age experience brings,
    We find that cats can't calculate,
      And ravens *don't* steal rings.
Pray what has become of it? Why did it go?'
And what I'm to answer I'm sure I don't know!

I'm certain to hear of it all day long;
And it's doubly unpleasant, when nothing's gone wrong,
To be scolded as if you'd been coming it strong!
Oh, the least little slip, were it never so small,
Were fifty times better than nothing at all!'

PART II.

Baron von Stein
Came of a line
As long as you'll easily find on the Rhine :—
(Strong words, by the way,
For I know, to this day,
A Mainzer whose castle, I've twice heard him say,
Was 'three times in mortgage ere Adam grew gray;'
And gravely explain that 'in birthright and blood,
Mere *parvenu* families date from the flood;')—
Such a smart cavalier
Never handled a spear,
Nor tossed off a schoppin of mighty Bock-bier;
And his auburn moustache went right over his ear;
So it's needless to add, what you've probably guessed,
That he owned the best part of each feminine breast,
Like 'the young Lochinvar that came out of the west!'

Baron von Stein in his balcony sate,
Smoking his porcelain pipe:
Nothing particular filled his pate,
For mischief ever too ripe!
In capital cue
For the gentleman who
Likes to find idle folks plenty to do,
And sets them to work with ineffable *goût*,
Just as bad little boys are employed by a Jew!

As a point of 'costume,'
You'll agree, I presume,
The pipe is a fact I may fairly assume;
Though I well recollect that some innocent blockhead
Makes Raleigh bring home the first 'clay' in his pocket,
And much flabbergaster the courtiers all,
By leisurely blowing his cloud at Whitehall;
Till James cried, 'Wal'r it gars me speak,
But the Deil's ainsel could-na bide this reek;
Ye'll find your head croppit, mon, just in a week!'
   The fact and the date
   I leave to their fate;
And boldly assert that I'd rather relate
The lyingest myth of a sea-snake and merman,
Than hoax all my friends with a pipeless young German!

  Well, there he sat smoking,
  When, suddenly croaking,
 A raven dropped from out of the sky,
  And perched on the rail,
  Wagging his tail,
And winking away with a blood-shot eye.

   A raven—a fright!
   Its eyes were alight
With a horrid red glow, and its tail wasn't tight,
And its beak was all wrong, and its feathers weren't right,
And its croak was obscene, and it smelt of the night,
And its manners were horribly strange and polite.
 For, hop! it stood on the Baron's shoe,
  And dropped a strange old ring,
 As much as to say, 'There's a trifle for you!
 Don't ask any questions: they're useless. Adieu!'

Then flapped its rusty wing;
And ere Baron von Stein
Got further than ' Mein——!'
That shocking black raven was over the Rhine!

Our bold Engineers,
In the field, it appears,
As a rule, run away with their thumbs in their ears
When the powder's all right,
And the slow-match alight,
Some hideous infernal-machine to ignite;
And, safe in the rear, growing valorous quite,
See the sky full of Frenchmen with martial delight!
Just so, to my thinking, it's perfectly plain
That, raven or devil, he's lighted *his* train;
And, finding his plot need no further assistance,
Sneaked off to enjoy the good fun from a distance.

But it's time to return to our poor Ermengarde,
Whom we left, you know, shocked and hysterical;
Very fairly complaining, 'twas cruelly hard
To be ruined off-hand by a miracle.
In vain did her maidens to calm her essay,
And assure her that they
Were ready to say,
And swear and declare upon oath any day,
That the ring—not the lady—had wandered astray;
That the Count was to blame;
And a sin and a shame
It was to try on such a treacherous game;
And he wasn't a man; and they hoped for that same
He'd get knocked on the head, which would settle *his* claim,
And leave his poor lady in peace and fair fame!

On topics like these they descanted until
They found they were wasting their balm and their skill,
And perceived that a further investment of breath
Would be simply to frighten their mistress to death ;
When, just as we've seen, in some gay pantomime,
Some 'Genius of Discord,' or 'Monster of Crime,'
Descend in red flame, with a fifty-man roar,
Amid thunder and smoke, through a smutty trap-door,
As a nice little fairy, all spangle and wings,
Floats in, on almost imperceptible strings,
To request that the clouds will at once disappear,
Because Beauty's triumphant and Virtue is clear—
So Ermengarde started at hope's bright gleam,
And her little heart leapt like a trout in a stream,
As in rushed a blooming soubrette with a scream :—

'O ma'am ! dear ma'am ! what a fortunate thing !
Here's a strapping young gentleman's found the ring !
And I says, ma'am, says I, ' Now you mustn't come in '
But he winks, and chucks me under the chin.
O ma'am ! dear ma'am ! how ever he dares !—
Here's the strapping young gentleman coming up stairs !'

' Dear lady, I feel that your pardon is mine,'
Said the bland, irresistible Baron von Stein ;
  'To be able to bring
  Good news of your ring
Is—in short, it's a most satisfactory thing !
  And I'm certain you'll pay
  In a liberal way,
The trifle I ask for my trouble to-day :
Three kisses—but three !—from those exquisite lips,
And safe on your finger the article slips.

I know you'll be startled. You'll say, 'What ! no more ?
Dear Baron, take six !—take a dozen—a score !
I never felt really grateful before !'
And fairly admit it's excessively handsome
To claim, after all, such a nominal ransom !'

'Three kisses ! Not one, Sir !" said brave Ermengarde ;
  'Good gracious !
   Audacious !
  Begone, Sir !—for shame !
And think yourself lucky to go as you came !
If you *do* keep the ring, Sir, remember you've stolen it ;
And my husband shan't rest till your skin's got a hole in it !'
   * * * * * *

  With angry cheek and sparkling eye,
   The proud young Ermengarde
  Watched the wild Baron thunder by,
   Across the castle-yard,
  And spur his charger savagely
   Among the drawbridge-guard.

  The warders fled, in snarling dread,
   From his horse-hoofs' fiery clatter ;
  But they stopped his groom, and punched his head
   To find out what was the matter.

'Three kisses, indeed ! (that's a beautiful mare !)
 He's rather mistaken in me !
(The wretch rides uncommonly well, I declare,)
 And may wait a long while for his fee !
Three kisses, indeed ! (what a lovely moustache !)
 The trumpery ring he may keep ;
(I needn't, perhaps, have been quite so harsh ;)
 It won't much trouble my sleep !

For this twelvemonth to come he's quite welcome to wear it;
Till then, goodness knows, I can easily spare it!'
    So Ermengarde cried,
    In matronly pride,
And the ring, and the Count, and the Baron defied,
And declared it was equally wrong and absurd
To be worried to death by the freak of a bird,
And that nothing on earth should induce her to care
For a ring that she felt it quite shameful to wear!

    Alas! that night,
    Long before light,
She started and woke in a deuce of a fright,
    For her dreams had been
    Of a dreadful scene,
Where a raw-headed Count, with a mangled mien,
On a three-legged horse—with never a Squire—
Battered and bloody, and black with mire;
His breastplate burst, and his shirt on fire,
    Rode wearily towards the gate;
Hailing his towers with:—'Ermengarde!
Here I am back again, pummelled and scarred,
With my pockets picked and my brain-pan starred;
Jogging away to a strange church-yard!
My Ring!—my Ring! It's cruelly hard
    To make a dead man wait!'
So the course of her thoughts, as it's easy to see,
Ran easily on from the ring to—the fee.

    'Had he asked me for *one*,
    In friendship or fun,
It isn't unlikely I might have said 'done!'
One kiss! Why it's over before it's begun!
I'm sure that it needn't astonish a nun!

Had he asked me for *two*,
I might have said 'Pooh!
You're asking too much, sir! That never will do!'
But then, even then—why, the beautiful hue
Of that curly moustache might have carried one through
Without even fainting—unless people knew
Some pleasanter method of bringing one to
Than that horrid cold water which wets one all through.
But THREE!
Dear me,
It's a frightful fee!
Oh, no! it's absurd to expect I'll agree.
And yet, by the way, had he asked me for ten,
What would three have looked, by comparison, then?'

So an innocent, pink little three-cornered note
Went off at break of day;
Its terms I'd be only too happy to quote,
But I really mustn't delay.
It went in the boot of an orderly Lancer,
With orders by all means to 'wait for an answer.'

The answer came, as you may divine,
In bodily shape of the Baron von Stein,
Who had got himself up so excessively fine
That he looked like Hyperion going to dine,
Or a 'gent' stepped out of a valentine.

'Dear lady,' said he,
'Though I plead for my fee,
Believe me, I'm willing as willing can be
That business and pleasure should ever agree.

I need not say,
One's debts to pay
By easy instalments is far the best way ;
So, by your kind leave, I'll take one kiss to-day ;
To-morrow one more ;
And clear off my score
The day after that, when the ring I restore.
Will you kindly permit me, when quite at your leisure,
To score off one-third of the price of your treasure ? '

* * * * * *

I find with regret,
That the ancient MS.
I've consulted as yet
With such signal success,
Grows here quite illegible : O such a mess !
What with nasty black thumbs,
And tobacco, and crumbs,
I can't for the life of me make out what comes ;
And it's doubly a nuisance to find that one's losing
What people have thought so extremely amusing.
The fact is, I'm floored ; and I only creep on
Through the help of the under-librarian at Bonn—
A kind, clever person, whose name I'd be glad
To publish in capital letters, and add
How much he assists me my task to surmount ;
But he begs that I won't, upon any account.

Our version is this :—
That the very first kiss
Was not, after all, taken greatly amiss ;
And, after the second, we both agree,
The Baron decidedly stayed for tea ;
And, after the third, as we quite understood,
The Baron undoubtedly stayed for good !

Or rather, till somebody hinted, one day,
Of an elderly gentleman jogging that way,
All tattered, and battered, and grimy, and gray,
As if he'd had rather more thumps than pay ;
When, to save explanations, in case of a call,
He mizzled one morning, ring, lady, and all !

  The Count came back from Jericho
   In fearful frame of mind,
  For since he marched, a year ago,
   The Fates had been unkind ;
   And right upon his beaver,
   A rampant Unbeliever
Had hit him such a vicious chop with something like a cleaver,
As quite unshipped his figure-head, and left him in a fever ;
And some one else had knocked him down and trod upon
  his face,
And started his rib-timbers with a big barbaric mace :
   And the surgeons, in their mystery,
    Had come up in the wake ;
   For he'd eaten half a blister, he
    Declared, through their mistake
   And, in scooping out an arrow
    That came from a Turk's quiver,
   They'd pricked his spinal marrow
    And cut him in the liver.
And rations had been scanty, and he'd lived on toads and roots,
And made a little bouilli of his bridle and his boots ;
And, in short, he was with fortune altogether out of suits.

   And when at last his gates he reached,
    With dim old 'scutcheons graven,
   'Tis said above him sat and screeched
    A horrid rusty raven ;

And when he found that knocking
   Brought no one to the door,
'Tis said, as if in mocking,
   The raven screeched the more ;
Till his fury grew quite shocking,
   And, good gracious, how he swore !

My tale is nearly ended, and there's little more to add,
Except that in a week or so the Count went barking mad,
And took to biting people's legs, a joke extremely bad ;
Until at last, reluctantly, they had to buy a padlock,
And chain him up to ruminate alone upon his bad luck.
And so he lived, I think they say, about another year,
Growing dull and apathetic—putting spiders in his beer,
And playing at cat's-cradle, till his end drew very near ;
And then he roused a little, but he hadn't much to say,
And hadn't time to say it, for he died that very day.

And when they came to bury him, a raven, all the while,
Sat by, and croaked and chuckled in a most provoking style;
   Which seemed so bad a sign,
   That they bribed a sleek divine
To light a pound of candles once a week upon the shrine
Of every saint whose patronage extended to the Rhine ;
And sing him safe, if possible, with masses ninety-nine !

PETER AND TULIP.

A LEGEND OF BERGEN-OP-ZOOM.

CLEAR shone the moonlight on windmill and tree,
By the dykes and the dunes of the deep Zuyder Zee;
As there, by the shore, on a shaggy sea-stone,
Sat Peter and Tulip—two lovers—alone.

Let us talk, first of all, about Tulip's papa,
Who was stout—as the Dutch not unfrequently are :
    A smooth, quiet man,
    Of whom the tale ran
That once in his life he concocted a plan
For secretly smuggling Dutch cheese to Japan,
And chartered a schooner at once, and began.

You'll remember the myth of a certain Tycoon,
Who said it was clear as his uncle at noon,
That cheeses were part of his aunt—the old moon ;
And bade his good people abandon the habit
Of turning his ancestor into Welsh rabbit :—
Forbade them, in fact, to fetch cheese from the dairy,
On pain of a punishment called 'hari-kari.'

It was then—there's no doubt—
That Krinkel van Kraut,
Profoundly reflecting that Stilton to stout
Was a thing which no fellow could manage without,
Like Mercy's own angel, sailed in, and sailed out.

Well, the guilders he made
By this little trade,
Could scarcely, I'm told, have been counted or weighed!
Some guessed them at thousands—at millions, and so on,
Without any possible *data* to go on.

In a massive black box,
Like a coffin with locks,
His hard-gotten coin kept this cunning old fox.
His daily delight lay in bolting the door
And spilling some dozen big bags on the floor,
And shouting with joy, as he danced round the room,
' I'm the luckiest rascal in Bergen-op-Zoom!'

It is true, to be sure, that, for guarding his heap,
This lucky old gentleman never could sleep.
Bright off his bolster
(A sword-case and holster)
He'd start up at once, if he heard but a soul stir;
And wander till morning from attic to hall,
With a six-barrelled blunderbuss loaded with ball.
So watchful in fact that, when fairly awake,
He shot a policeman most nights by mistake.

'Twere idle to note
What stories afloat
Anent this old rogue were in every one's throat:—
What whispers went round,
When bumpers were crowned

By weather-worn skippers who nightly abound
At the time-honoured sign of 'The Galliot Aground;'
    What wagers were laid
      That Kraut, whilst in trade,
Had counted far less on the cheese he purveyed
To the coy Japanese, than on Somebody's aid,
Who formerly backed him in rapine and raid,
And, one day or other, would call to be paid—
A 'point' which was always received with applause,
And infinite clapping of heavy sea-paws.
Far better, methinks, had those jolly old salts
Thought less of his prospects, and more of his faults.

For my part, I'm silent. Above and below,
I've written down all that I really know.
I never do more, and I never do less;
No matter how Editors tease or caress.
I wouldn't, in short, for a forty-pound fee,
Write aught that I thought wasn't true to a T.

Miss Tulip, I'm happy to say, was a child
By none of the failings paternal defiled;
She was hardly sixteen, yet a nicer young lass
I truly believe never looked in a glass.
Her figure was certainly only tol-lol,
And her face like the face of a rosy wax doll:
    But as for her waist,
      That's matter of taste,
And beauties in Dutch-land are seldom incased
In corslets—or else very tenderly laced.
And where grow such kisses as those which we take
From cheeks which are handsomely tinted with lake?

So Tulip had lovers, what lady has not,
Who's pa keeps a locker so brimful of shot,
With none but herself to lay hold of the lot
Whenever dry Death may away with him trot?
Besides, recollect what a regular Paradise
Sea-sodden Holland to ladies unmarried is.
Think of the ships that incessantly touch,
Landing amorous crews at the quays of the Dutch;
And you'll feel that their proverb, 'More suitors, more sport,'
Quite suits that Low Country of naval resort.

  So here is a list
  Of people who kissed
Miss Tulip's white fingers, and couldn't exist
If so be as they mightn't lay hold of her fist:
Imprimis—A lovely black Frenchman from Paris;
Item—A freshman from Cambridge, called Harris;
Item—A Russian, who smelt like a pill;
Item—A German, whom beer couldn't fill;
Item—A Spaniard, who pricked his Toledo
Through Item, a Turk, for confounding his credo:
And, Item, a Dane, who fought over his can
With Item, a great howling Irishman.
And more I dare say. What a catalogue's this!
What work for a poor little painstaking miss,
Who smiled upon all—though she kept a far sweeter
Constriction of oscular muscle for Peter.

Our Peter built boats, by the brink of the Scheldt,
And hammered the louder the more that he felt.
When tranquil, he'd whistle, and tap to the tune,
From the cool rosy morn to the dark afternoon.
When rampant with love, and Miss Tulip desiring,
His hammer-work sounded like heavy file firing!

Now, but for this temper, so wild and unequal,
We might have been spared a deplorable sequel:
But here we go back to that shaggy sea-stone,
Where last we left Peter and Tulip alone.

I know not exactly what compliments passed;
I know there was precious hard hugging at last;
I know that next morning our Peter flew straight
To Krinkel's old house, in the Vanderclootz Gate,
Bounced into the room where that rascal was dressing,
And cried:—
       'Sir, I'm Tulip's, and ask for your blessing!'

I would that my pen were a pencil to seize
The face of that ci-devant merchant of cheese!
He seldom said much, till he'd scanned you awry
With a parrot-like leer of his crooked old eye;
And then, if he fancied you worth a reply,
You got it in 'chaff,' most annoyingly dry.

'My Peter,' he said, 'you're aware, I presume,
I'm the deafest old rascal in Bergen-op-Zoom.
I'm deafer than ever to-day—quite unable
To hear, if you talked like the Tower of Babel.
Good day.'
      'Sir,' said Peter, 'your jokes are delightful,
But think of my feelings—they're perfectly frightful!
You've standing before you a desperate man, Sir,
Who comes upon business, and waits for an answer.'

     'Oh, ho!' said Mynheer;
     'I fancy I hear
One little piece more than I did—but, O dear!
This deafness is dreadful. You tell me, I think,
Barge-building don't find you in 'baccy and drink;

That Tulip's a few little florins to clink;
And, if you could only the governor sink,
Life's colour would always be perfectly pink.
Now, mark me:—So long as I'm able to crawl,
I don't mean my Tulip to marry at all.
A girl, to my mind, is a donkey, or worse,
Who parts, for a fool, with her person and purse.
That's all. When I die you may dance on my grave,
And carelessly spend what I carefully save.
Till then you can wait. You perceive the slight barrier?'

Cried Peter: 'I'll do what you mention, and marry her!
You smiling old sinner, I solemnly swear,
That, when to the churchyard at last you repair,
I'll pull on my pumps, and I'll follow you there,
And dance on your tombstone all night, you old bear!'

'You may dance off your drumsticks for all that I care,'
Said Krinkel van Kraut—and so parted the pair.

*   *   *   *

At last the time came for old Kraut to fall ill.
The doctors drew round him, to cure or to kill;
And they killed him at last;—but he first made his will.

He wrote it, verbatim, as follows:—

'AMEN.
Vrouw Tulip's a great deal too fond of young men.
They're all much alike—but especially Peter;
Who'd pocket her cash, on condition he'd eat her;—
I therefore devise and bequeath her as little
Of mine, as may keep her in lodging and victual;
Say guilders five hundred per annum, paid quarterly,—
So long as she hates the said Peter most mortally.

The rest, I request, may be spent on my tomb :—
I wish the said Peter went there in my room!—
I'd have it be built of black marble and brass,
With handsome large figures, that people who pass
May think of old Kraut, as he lies in the grass.
I give what remains, after building this tomb,
To the Nine Greatest Rascals in Bergen-op-Zoom—
Expressly providing, that of it no penny
Shall reach the said Peter—the greatest of any.
That's all. I've said all that I'm likely to say.
I don't leave a debt that I'm anxious to pay.
I've done a good bit that was doubtful no doubt,
But business is business :—
     'Hoop Krinkel van Kraut.'

This precious performance he ended, and eyed
With a great deal of pleasure and scholarly pride.
 'Not one man in ten,
  When he took up his pen,
Would have hoisted all sail, and begun with Amen!'
He muttered : 'Confound them, those counsellors itch
To make their works read like the prayer of a witch,
That pays out stern-foremost with never a hitch,
So I've dipped my brush in the right pot of pitch!'
Perhaps he was right, and the lawyers were wrong,
Who fancied he'd 'pitched it' a little too strong,
And pitchforked his will with a Chancery prong.

The point was a fine one, and famous good sport
It made for a week in the Chancellor's Court.
Nine dozen Great Rascals had claimed the bequest ;
Each burning to prove he out-rascalled the rest :
'Till Justice, incensed at their odious details,
Should have flogged them all into the street with her scales.

Twelve eminent counsel, tremendous in horsehair,
Fought over their prey, like the crew of a Corsair.
' Could the Court—for the point was exceedingly small—
Pronounce upon whom the bequest was to fall ?
Would my Lord the grim office of jackal assume
To the Nine Greatest Rascals in Bergen-op-Zoom ?
Or, granting that course too flagitiously funny,
Decide as to what must be done with the money?'

Great guns of the law make tremendous reports,
In which they put all that occurs in our courts;
And the lore which these calf-covered Korans contain
Is food for the faithful—in Chancery Lane.

In Holland, I'm told, a like practice prevails ;
Which tempts me at once to dispense with details.
   I'd rather you'd look
   In the regular book,
Where everything's hashed by a Chancery-cook.
You'll find the whole story reported in Dutch
(A language I'm certain you'll like very much),
The statement—the pleadings—the judgment and all.
In sentences worthy of Westminster Hall.

The Judge did his duty : he never gave tongue
Till every one's rattle had fairly been sprung.
   Then woke up and said,
   'The testator was dead—?'
(Twelve eminent counsel each nodded a head ;)
Remarked more than once, 'there was something in *that;*'
Propounded from Grotius passages pat ;
Pronounced for a tomb of black marble and brass ;
Dismissed the Nine Rascals at once, as a class ;

Considered Miss Tulip's an absolute gift;
Suggested she needn't send Peter adrift;
Opined that the clause about 'hating' before him
Was palpably void—merely meant '*in terrorem ;*'
Then placidly named the potential enjoyers
Of residue—long ago gone to the lawyers.

Sombre in aspect, and sable in hue,
Slowly that ponderous monument grew.
Four-square and firm was the pedestal wrought
In smooth, shining marble from Sicily brought:
Cold couch for a statue—but there, high and dry,
Lay Krinkel van Kraut with his toes to the sky;
So carefully carved, that it seemed like himself,
In Sunday-go rigging, asleep on a shelf.
One hand seemed to toy with a ball of Dutch cheese,
The other, a bag of Dutch guilders to squeeze;
Whilst, fringing him round, a quaint legend imparted
Good news to the friends of the pious departed.

Four cardinal virtues stood, one at each corner,
Partly as trumpeter, partly as mourner.
Each a brass trumpet stood ready to blow;
Each had a brazen face beaming with woe.
Each bore a hand at supporting the weight
Of the massive black slab-stone or canopy-plate,
Which poised over Kraut may, for all that I know,
Have made it extremely snug lying below.

So Peter and Tulip were blessed in their lot;
The present was pleasant—the past was forgot.
Their prospects, though blighted by long litigation,
Were fair enough, quite, for young folks in their station.
Barge-building was brisk; and the clink of *one* hammer
Had never before made such musical clamour.

'Rap-a-tap, tap! what a lucky chap this is—
Rap-a-tap, tap! to get so many kisses—
Rap-a-tap, tap! from a girl so divine—
Rap-a-tap, tap! and, to-morrow, she's mine!
Then at misfortune my fingers I'll snap:
Rap-a-tap!—tap-a-tap!—tap-a-tap! Tap!
Tap!'

    Song and hammer and barge were forgot;
And Peter stood silent, all flustered and hot,
As if a stray nail had nailed him to the spot.

Alas! he remembered that this was the night
For keeping a vow made in anger and spite.
To-morrow, in wedlock, dear Tulip he took;
To-night on the tombstone a leg must be shook.
I wish I could say—but it wouldn't be true—
He very much wished his rash oath to undo.
I fear that his hatred of Kraut was too deep;
I fear that he burned his appointment to keep;
I fear the wild act had a fierce fascination,
A desperate pleasure—a dreadful temptation—
Like that which induces, when evenings grow damp,
A mild fussy moth to fly into the lamp.

He pondered but little—the night was fast falling;
The weather-wise cranes from the roof-tops were calling;
The rain-clouds were winging in troops through the sky;
And then he strode off, with 'I'll do it, or die!'

The night grew far worse ere he reached the churchyard!
The floodgates of heaven seemed fairly unbarred;
The rain fell in torrents—the waves came ashore,
In the fast-rising gale with a ponderous roar.

The moon hid her crescent, or glared with a light
Which blurred and disfigured that horrible night;
While, seaward, the rumble of guns through the gloom
Told of coasters in trouble off Bergen-op-Zoom.

But Peter strode on, for his courage was good:
At last in the churchyard of Bergen he stood.
A wild hurried moon-gleam swept over the grass,
And lit up the grave of black marble and brass;
And there, on the slab-stone, while boldly advancing
His oath to fulfil—*he saw somebody dancing!*

O Peter, why didn't you bolt like a shot!
What made you creep stealthily up to the spot?
What made you look on, with those great open eyes,
At what you saw there?—it was worse than unwise.
It is, I've been told, a most grievous mistake
For little birds ever to look at a snake.
There's a force in that changeless and passionless eye
Which no little bird ever hatched can defy.
They gaze, and they gaze, till at last, in dismay,
They chirp ' O good gracious, we can't fly away!'
So fared it with Peter, when once he began
To gaze, like a dunce, at that little old man.

For little he seemed, yet as lithe as a cat;
In face like a wicked and battered old bat;
With an odd sort of smile on his lips of black leather,
Which made him an odd sort of cove altogether.

He didn't seem worse for the wind or the rain,
But whistled, and chuckled, and danced might and main.
Now bounding, his fingers he merrily snapped,
Now falling, his' toes on the tombstone he tapped;

Now, shaking with mirth, he spun round like a top,
And high into air again went with a hop.
He must, Peter thought, have got quite in a heat,
For little blue sparks crackled under his feet.
At last he stopped short :—
                        ' My good boy, are you there ?
Why, Peter, you've got on your pumps, I declare !
Did you come here to dance in this delicate weather ?
You did ! Well, how lucky ! We'll both dance together !
Nice gale, is it not ? Blowing dead upon shore !
It's perfect enjoyment to waltz to the roar !
Jump up : here's my hand at your service—'
                                            Alas !
That Peter should ever have left the wet grass,
To stand on that grave of black marble and brass !
The moon hid her light in an instant, and—boom !
A wild peal of thunder broke over the tomb,
And rang and rebounded through Bergen-op-Zoom.
Since then, in the market—the trekschuit—the train—
Our Peter has always been looked for in vain.

That night over Holland it blew such a gale
As made even seafaring persons to quail.
        Whole forests were thinned
        And people were skinned
Alive in their boots by that horrid high wind.
But, what is more frightful, I find it averred
That, high over Bergen, a screeching was heard,
In tones which were clearly not those of a bird.

'Twas plain some poor person, who wanted to stay,
That night was borne bodily bawling away.
        But wherefore and where,
        Through storm-troubled air,

That victim of kidnap was borne in despair,
Or who, at the time, had him under his care,
I give you my honour I am not aware.
Wild guesses were made ; but of these, for the sake
Of poor little Tulip, no mention I'll make.
More light on the point I'm unable to throw :
I've written down all that I really know.

DOOM OF THE BRIEFLESS

PART I.

O, I am a-weary of Pumpkin Court,
    Its flags are hateful all to me!
Other men's chambers by clients are sought,
    To mine comes never the ghost of a fee!

My clerk sits in his mouldy den
    Gloomily biting his nails,
Or vacantly drawing of skeleton men,
    With goggle-eye faces and tails.

There are two that he's always a-drawing of nights,
    And I hear him snort with glee,
As down in the corner the rascal writes,
    'That's master—t'other man's me!'

He knows that each knock is the knock of a dun,
Or that some little dirty boy's done it in fun.
'Ah, knuckle away till your knuckles is sore,'
Says he: 'what's the good of *our* minding the door?'
So it isn't worth while for a cove to call,
And nobody, now-a-days, knocks at all!

I once was told,
By a gipsy bold,
(She scanned my palm on Epsom wold,)
That I should have more than my pockets would hold,
Round red sovereigns, clinking gold!
Says she, 'The first of next July,
I'm shot if your happiness won't run high,
For it's just about then that the starch will fly
  From out of your virgin wig!
   Though now you're poor,
    Your luck's as sure
  As the knife to a Christmas pig!
There's a lady as loves you that's fair and tall:
Stand us a quartern, and hear it all!'

  She lied, the jade! A lighter fee
  Had brought me, 'by return, post free,'
  A princely fortune in the Three
   Per Cents, from Joseph Ady![1]
  She lied! The glorious first is here,
  And longer grows the fell arrear,
  And clients none at all appear,
   Let alone the fair young lady!

  * * * * *

The clock had struck ten, and I sat me a-down
In the species of study distinguished as 'brown.'
'I'm the very unluckiest beggar in town,'
Cried I, 'in the darkness of Destiny's frown.'

---

[1] Joseph Ady's name is no longer the household word which it was when these lines were written. Any one who may be curious concerning the acts of this impostor and all that he did, will find the same recorded in the useful and entertaining columns of Chambers' *Book of Days*, vol. i. p. 616.

> When, hark! I declare,
> A step on the stair!
> (I forgot to remark that my rooms are three-pair;)
> At once, from my toes to the tips of my hair,
> I started and wondered, for visitors there,
> At that time of night, were remarkably rare:
> Still greater the shock
> When a sharp double knock
> Came, bang! like a pistol gone off at half-cock,
> And I heard my clerk shuffle his way to the lock,
> To see which of my duns had come this way to mock.
>
> They laugh!
> They chaff!
> I'd sooner by half
> They'd come in and bleed me at once, like a calf!
> Louder they chatter, and laugh the more,
> And now my clerk's in a regular roar;
> Then, bursting in
> With a handful of 'tin,'
> 'O master,' he shouted, 'here *is* a begin!
> I'd give a good pound now to be in your skin,
> I'm shot if I wouldn't! O shake us a fin!
> Ten guineas! Ten guineas! O my, what a game!
> Count 'em backwards or forwards they're always the same!
> And master! O master! the best of the job,
> See here! by the poker, they've tipped me five bob!
> If it isn't a BRIEF
> I'll be scragged for a thief!
> O! ain't we just going to shake out a reef!'
>
> I roared, I sighed,
> I laughed, I cried,
> And opened my eyes so excessively wide

You'd really have thought I must wear 'em outside,
And couldn't have shut 'em again if I tried.
I fell on the neck of my trusty boy
With a wild, wild hug of convulsive joy;
('Hi! master!' says he, 'don't you strangle my throat!')
And blubbered a cataract over his coat.
With tingling fingers I counted the gold,
And ten bright, round, red sovereigns told!
Then eagerly, wildly tore the tape,
That girdled my white brief's beautiful shape.

I glanced it through, and found that Roe
Had grievously injured the harmless Doe—
Wounded him, battered him, torn his coat,
And pitched him into a castle moat;
Pulled him out, and pummelled him more,
Pinched him, and kicked him behind and before;
Gouged him, scalped him, trod on his toes,
Pushed in his eye-tooth and pulled off his nose,
Flattened his head—to wit, with a spade—
And nicked his ribs—to wit, with a blade—
Till Doe couldn't anyway work at his trade,
And was cruelly sick, and extremely afraid;
And every stiver he had in the till
Had gone to settle the doctor's bill!
All which merely meant, that, while over their beer,
They'd quarrelled; when Doe got a box on the ear;—
The rest being simply *ad libitum* readings,
To make the case neat and compact on 'the pleadings.'

  I saw myself in Fancy's glass
  Stand forth with front of triple brass;
  I saw the Judge, I saw the Jury,
  I saw the plaintiff green with fury;

I heard my own hot eloquence
Denounce in thunder the defence,
Proclaim the perjured rascal, Roe,
And ask him where he thought he'd go !
And then, oh, then, the wild applause
That told me I had gained my cause ;
While with tumultuous cheers came blent
The Judge's well-turned compliment !
I heard it—saw it—felt it all !
Could pride like this deserve a fall ?

Two friends I had, and only two,
Barring pawnbrokers many, and bailiffs a few ;
Two friends I had, who both, like me,
Knew seldom a visitor—never a fee.
Bright was the vision of 'supper for three !'

'Fly, fly, brave youth, to Temple Square,
You know George Samuel Brown lives there,
Give him my compliments, say, "can he spare,
Two hours this evening to muzzle old Care ?"
And further fly, brave Ariel, still,
And be careful to say that it *isn't* a bill
When you ask Augustus Smith if he will
Be with me this evening a bumper to fill ?
We'll meet at the "Rainbow ;" and, Ariel, stay !
   Visit, I pray,
   Without delay,
That excellent woman, my laundress,[1] and say
I'd thank her this moment to toddle this way.
For boiling a kettle, and setting a tray,

---

[1] 'Laundress,' in Temple nomenclature, is the style and title of the venerable female whose duties correspond with those of a college 'bedmaker.'

I don't know her equal; and toddy to supper
Comes natural as to the saddle the crupper,
That's all!' He flew! My laundress came,
Hoping as how that I didn't make game
Of a poor old soul as was widdi'd and lame.

   'Dear me, Mrs. Jones,
    Do spare your groans,'
Says I, ' 'tisn't I would have troubled your bones;
But the fact is, good woman, my grandmother's dead,
And has left lucky Briefless to reign in her stead!
   So quick, Mrs. J.,
    Step over the way
To the "Nine Happy Niggers," and civilly say
I'll thank 'em to lend me both tumblers and tray,
For I've company coming and mean to be gay;
We sup at the "Rainbow"—chops, kidneys, and beer;
But our grog, Mrs. Jones, we intend to take here.
So I'll thank you to see that the decks are all clear,
   The tumblers all bright,
    And the fire alight,
With a fizzing hot kettle by twelve this night!'

Oh, wasn't the dingy old lady struck dumb
When I tipped up the change for a bottle of rum!
   She eyed me askance
    With a doubtful glance,
As round my arm-chair I continued to dance;
And says, ' Mr. B., sir, I hope, to be sure,
You ain't been a stealing what never was your'?
Recollect, sir, it wasn't no sin to be poor.'

   I calmed her scruples: told a lie,
   I've not the slightest notion why;

Remarked old people often die
    And leave their cash behind 'em.
Why upon earth I couldn't say,
'The simple fact is, Mrs. J.,
I've got my maiden brief to-day,'
    Or why I lied at random,
I know not now—I never knew:
I burst away—I ran, I flew!
Dim visions, yet, around me cling
Of that wild night: we did the thing!
The very waiters formed a ring
    And laughed with greasy glee,
As chop and steak and kidney fled,
And still the gleaming tankard sped
From bar to board, and still we fed
    And drank like whirlpools three!
    And then, in my pride,
    'My bricks,' I cried,
'I needn't inform you with me it's high tide,
And the tin's running in; but I bet you guess wide,
And wouldn't say *how* in a month if you tried,
    So shoot as you may!'
    Says Brown, 'I'd lay
A trifle you've spotted a winner to-day.'
Said Smith, 'I think he's nabbed a thief
With a whacking reward!' 'No,' says I, 'it's a BRIEF!'

    'A BRIEF! No, no!
    Come, *that's* no go!
We'll pound it you haven't a paper to show!
Not likely now, is it?' I laughed, ho, ho!
'Come to my chambers, you'll find Doe and Roe
A Brief and three tumblers all in a row!
We'll wet the Brief, we'll count my wealth,
And drink a future Lord Chancellor's health!'

'Agreed, agreed!'
The waiter was fee'd ;
We left him very much pleased indeed :
We rushed all three at the Temple Gate,
Gloomily frowning in midnight state ;
We knocked the knock of a lunatic mob,
To waken the porter asleep on his hob.
Methought a reverent glance he wore,
And bowed as he never had bowed before ;
' 'Tis well !' said I ; ' those practised eyes
Detect a Chancellor on the rise !'

Clattering up the lamp-lit stair,
We rushed like madmen, as we were,
We burst into the old ' three-pair ;'
The fire was blazing, the glasses were bright,
The jolly old grog-bottle laughed in the light !
The kettle was fizzing 'By George, it's all right !'
We chuckled, and all, in our happiest tones,
Broke out in a chorus of ' Good Mrs. Jones !'

' Good Mrs. Jones ' came curtseying in—
' They hadn't no rum, so I've brought you gin,'
Says she, ' and the table is nicely laid,
And see what a capital fire I've made !
That great paper faggot has served its turn—
It's right in the middle !   Oh, didn't it burn !'

' Ye Gods,' I roared, ' for death's relief !
O Heaven and Earth !—MY VIRGIN BRIEF !'

THE FINALE.

O, for an organ—and an organist,
    To growl me smothered thunder :—then to pour
All that of sound and fury may consist ;
    A salvo such as never crashed from score !—
    Splinter the window-panes and split the floor !
I was an eagle murdered in the sky ;
    The rush and revel of my morning soar
Blasted and marred in sudden agony ;
While she who did the deed looked on with idiot eye !

What followed is a mazy dream ;
I think Jones fainted with a scream ;
I think Smith laughed—I think his head
I fiercely punched with fist of lead,
    And war-whoop wild and shrill !
I think Brown chaffed—I think he bled ;
I think both lip and nose ran red
    In one short fiery mill !

Yet, even this I wouldn't swear ;—
Until I breathed a purer air
Than blows through Pumpkin's dreary square,
    I only felt—undone !
One wretched serf indeed I met,
Upon whose brow my mark I set ;
He chafed me in my angry fret
    By bellowing ' Pa-st one !'

Enough of this! Through Temple Bar
  I rushed into the Strand;
A cabman shouted, 'Here you are!'
  He knew not that my hand
Was raised to curse my destiny,
And not to such a thing as he.

Far westward, towards Trafalgar-square,
A bull's eye pink, with sickly stare,
And lettered lines of bloodshot glare,
    Scowls on the midnight pave:
'And here,' I cried, 'is rest at last!
The lot is drawn, the die is cast,
And, swamped in Fortune's ruthless blast,
    Here Briefless claims a grave!
Come, true apothecary, come!
One penny roll with poisoned crumb,
One sleepy cup of hemlock numb—
    'Tis all the gift I crave!'

I rang a peal both long and loud
  Till I broke the night-bell handle,
And roused a man in a dimity shroud,
  With a night-cap and flat candle.

Out of the window his wrathful head
Came popping like Punch, as it bitterly said,
'What are you after, you groggy young swell,
A-jerking like that of my medical bell?
In a minnit or less you'll walk off to the cell.
Come! what do you want there, a-ringin' and drummin'?
If it *is* your good lady, I'm comin'? I'm comin'!'

'Come down!' I cried. 'Such need as mine
  Might rouse the Sleepers Seven;
Come down, if you *are* in the medical line;—
  Come down, for the love of Heaven!'

In went the head. With a clank and a clack,
A chain went down and a bolt went back;
    And a sharp little snout
    Came ferreting out,
With, 'What upon earth is this shindy about?
    Now then, sir, what is it?
    Who asked for this visit?
Are you drunk, sir—or dumb, sir? Come, pray be explicit.'

'I shouldn't have hit such a rat-tat-tat-tat,'
Says I, sobbing loud, 'but I don't keep a cat,
And what's the best poison to poison a rat?'

    If some sad ghost had risen,
      With cold blood in its veins,
    From subterranean prison,
      (Suppose the city drains,)
    And on the night-bell mournfully
      Tolled a slow minute-peal,
    And hailed the Doctor scornfully
      With face of glistening veal,
    And bade him to the shady
      Descend on rapid pins,
    Because a spectral lady
      Was lying in with twins—
I doubt if through his little breast
    The blood had bounded quicker,

Than when I broke upon his rest,
  In anguish and in liquor.

With shaded eyes and look amazed
Upon my face awhile he gazed,
And then I saw his rising bile
Melt in a strange yet pitying smile.
'Come in,' he said; and closed the door.
'A rat, you say?—his pranks are o'er.
  I quite understand;
  I'll take him in hand,
And I don't think his days will be long in the land.
There's nothing like arsenic—eh, sir?'
                                'By Jove!'
Cried I, 'but you *are* an intelligent cove!
That's just what I wanted.'
                        'Ha, ha! just so,'
Says he, 'only don't you go peaching, you know.
  For the Lord of Carlisle,
  Meddling old file,
Won't let us sell it, 'cause people *will* bile
It up with their puddin' their vitals to spile;
Unless, to be sure, there's a witness to look
And sign his name legible down in a book,
As much as to say, it shan't go to the cook.[1]
But with you, sir, I see that it can't go wrong;
So I'll mix you a dose of my superfine strong.
Don't say where you got it—that's all.' He took
An ill-looking canister out of a nook,
  Saying 'Ah, this rat's a martyr;
  He'll find he's caught a Tartar;

---

[1] *Vide* 14th and 15th Vict. c. 13. s. ii.

He'll wag his tail and wink his eye for just a minnit arter,
And then for kingdom-come he'll take a precious quick
    departur';
I reckon to his latter end you wouldn't walk him smarter,
Not if you caught him with a cat and hung him in a garter.
I'll mark the paper "Poison," sir, in case it's left about;
Good night! a shilling—thank you: it will answer, I've no
    doubt.'

    I leant my back against a wall,
    And swallowed the packet—string, paper and all.

        Woes of that memorable eve!
          Vain were my poet-skill
        Your tangled web again to weave,
          Or say how very ill
I grew. In vain I cried for death,
A hiccup shook my gasping breath;
I staggered on through square and street,
With sob and sigh of maudlin bleat,
And cursed the druggist for a cheat,
In language that I won't repeat;
    Until at length I stood
Beside a shining midnight lake,
'By George,' I cried, 'this bosom-ache
May now be cured and no mistake!
From life's vague dream at last I wake,
And here my thirst of glory slake,
    And quit the stage for good!'

    Pale floating gleams of liquid light
    Flashed out in broken circlets bright;
    The chequered sky, the black old trees
        Spun whirling round. A splash!—a dive!

A hum as of ten thousand bees,
   When somebody's upset the hive,
All came, and went, and came again.
I swam—I sank, in horrid pain;
And then, and not till then, I found
I'd just as lieve remain undrowned.
Once more I rose, and with a yelp
Like that of some devoted whelp,
I gasped and bubbled, 'Help! HELP! HELP!'

Alas! repentance came too late—
The very fishes mocked my fate:
In shoals they rose to tear their prize;
Their cold blunt noses in my eyes
Came dub, dub, dub! With eager bite
They tore my whiskers left and right,
And bit my fingers, nipped my nose,
And swarmed within my smaller clothes.
They dragged me down: I may have rolled
   With Clarence amid 'heaps of pearl,'
Anchors and jewels, sculls and gold;
   I only felt one dizzy whirl.
But, when I rose for time the last,
A shout along the midnight blast
Rang sharply, 'In the water, ho!
Sing out and tell us where to row!'

I answered not, for down my throat
The fish swam thick; but soon a boat,
With flying oars, and lantern slung
Athwart the bow, beside me swung.
The steersman shouted 'Slack, men—slack!'
And drove his boat-hook through my back.

Four stalwart oarsmen hauled me in,
And picked the fishes off my skin.
  ' Poor buffer,' said they,
   ' He's seen a bad day,
Them gudgeons has bitten his eyelids away ;
They've nibbled his ears off as close as can be,
And his nose is a sight for a sinner to see,
And he's bustin' with mud, and he's all in a shiver!
What made him souse into the Serpentine River?'

They pulled ashore—they laid me out ;
They rolled me up in a blanket stout :
They rubbed me down with a red-hot brick,
Delighted to find I could hollo and kick,
Then put me to bed full of brandy and bark,
Saying, 'There now, he'll wake up as fresh as a lark!'

The wretched morning dawned at length :
I woke, like Samson, shorn of strength.
A cramp-knot gnawed in every limb,
My eyes were very sore and dim,
Yet, somehow, still I seemed to swim,
To sink, to struggle, and to cry
For help. Where was I? whence—and why?

   Around my bed,
   I heard the tread
  Of several ' Royal Humanes,'
   Who patted my head,
   And cheerfully said
  ' We're amply repaid for our pains !
Perhaps, my dear sir, if you have a spare sovereign,
You'll pop it some day the Society's coffer in—
That's just as you please. There's a cab at the door.
And we'll see you safe home to the old third floor!'

They drove me home; and up the stair
They carried me safe, like Guy Fawkes, in a chair;
Till, on reaching the landing, the end of my journey,
I stood face to face with a wolfish attorney!

    I knew him well—'twas he from whom
        That fatal BRIEF of yesterday
    Came, like a thunderbolt of doom!
        I strove, in vain, to faint away.
''Tis gone!' I shrieked, ''tis burnt!—Accursed
Be Mrs. Jones! You know the worst!
Here, slam my head against the wall;
Put me out of the window, and leave me to fall;
Do, somebody, please—if it isn't too small.'
'Dear sir,' said the Wolf, ''tis no matter at all!
Pray, pray don't take on so—you fill me with sorrow:
My *dear* sir, I'll send you another to-morrow!'

        I stared in vain,
        For through my brain
Vague thoughts ran wild. 'Oh, pray explain,'
I gasped, 'I'm in such horrid pain!'

    Then gaily spoke that man of law,
        'You *had* an old godfather;
    But he has been scragged by a Turkey Bashaw,
        Until he's choky—rather!
    He lived beside the Ganges broad,
        That runs nigh old Calcutta;
    He used to eat bank-notes, good Lord!
        Between his bread-and-butter;
    Till, as I said, he died in cord,
        As dead as that there shutter.
They called his name, in their Indian slang,
Sir Tigery Peppery Ourang Outang.

Well, once, it should seem, when you might have been
Almost, I should fancy, too little to wean,
Sir Tigery came your father to see,
And gave you a ride on his shaky old knee,
Till you cried with delight—being partial to yellow—
'See father—oh see! what a beautiful fellow!'

' He never forgot it; your name went down
At once in his will for the uttermost ' brown.'
There's rupees in silver and mohurs in gold,
There's a hatful of pearls—value?—gad, it's untold!
There's consols by thousands, as good as a plum,
And a string of pink diamonds as big as your thumb
I wish you all joy, sir—life, happiness, health,
And *a sharp, honest agent* to manage your wealth;
My firm, I assure you, are proud as can be
To have found out your merit first—paid your first fee!
Long (of course) ere we knew you so luckily starred.
Good morning, sir! Stay—let me hand you my card!'

And was it all true? By the sun and the light,
'Twas true as could be, and the gipsy was right,
And Briefless has more than his pockets can hold,
Round red sovereigns, clinking gold!

POETRY VERSUS SCIENCE.

A FRESHMAN'S DREAM.

'Ne forte pudori
Sit tibi Musa lyræ solers, et cantor Apollo!'

You are a Cantab, reader, are you not?
   And did you dwell within the gates of Trinity?
I hope you did,—it is a pleasant spot;
   Besides, one claims and counts upon affinity
With those that erst have shared one's college lot;
   In fact it borders upon consanguinity:
Great thoughts expand;—By Jove! I wonder whether
We've ever smoked, dined, wined, or supped together?

Well, did you read? Perhaps it may have been your
   Luck to emerge in some immense Degree:
I scarcely dare imagine you were Senior
   Wrangler, but so it still perchance may be;
Perhaps you loved the Dons,—perhaps the Dean your
   Bosom companion may have been;—to me
He always bore a most unchristian spite:
I shot his cat,—and screwed him in one night.

Which he acknowledged by an imposition,
   Of grievous length:—I cut the whole concern.

Besides, about that time, I had a Vision ;
   As in some dozen stanzas you may learn,
Through Mr. Bentley's very kind permission ;
   So up the cataract of life return ;
Fancy it midnight :—hark, how sweetly swells
The stately chime of Great St. Mary's bells !

I closed old Euclid ;—for, within the grate,
   The dying flames their last faint flicker shed ;
Besides, the night was getting pretty late,
   Quite time for sober folk to be a-bed,
Who mean to grace the chapel-doors at eight,—
   A deed I always contemplate with dread ;
For man must roost, as well as go to church ;
And clings, at cock-crow, rather to the perch.

Still I sat on, to ponder o'er the past,
   The present, and the future, wondering long
For what ill deed my lot had thus been cast
   Amid dame Granta's stiff and solemn throng,
Chained to her dull, disheartening lore ;—at last
   I gave the matter up, and, right or wrong,
Vowed that I would, eschewing *pros* and *cons*,
Recross for ever 'Asinorum Pons.'

True 'bridge of sighs,'—infernal diagram !
   The boyish tears of generations dead
Thy cruel arch of woe conspire to damn !
   Cane, birch and block, boxed ears and aching head,
And sleepless nights, and days of weary cram,
   Lie all embodied in thine emblem dread !
But, to return :—I tumbled in :—to sleep
I went, and going, snored both loud and deep.

How long I slept I know not, 'till a sound
    Of gentle music trembled through the gloom;
I woke, or thought I woke, and gazed around,
    And, through the shadows of the darkened room,
Caught a dim outline, fresh and fair and round,
    Unlike the withered wanderers of the tomb
That come in ghostly garment, now and then,
To frighten sinful single gentlemen.

Such maidens as 'unfortunate Miss Bailey;'
    Who left the beaten path of love-lorn martyrs,
And, deeming she had acted somewhat frailly,
    Domestically perished in her garters;
Yet rose to dun the naughty captain daily,
    Or rather nightly, in his country quarters,
Until her small account was paid in paper;
Wherewith she vanished with a ghostly caper.

'False Ferdinand' had also to 'come down,'[1]
    Though not exactly with a one-poun' note,
Which doubtless he had paid by cheque on town,
    Could that have saved him from the spectre-boat:
Yet why this green Lothario chose to drown,
    To please a silly ghost, I can't make out;
Had it been me, I'd have shammed deaf and dumb;
Or told her roundly that I couldn't come.

There's nothing in this world that can compare
    With a good conscience: though, I almost think,
A sound digestion—now almost as rare,—
    (Which helps to form the comfortable link

---

[1] 'Come down, false Ferdinand, for whom I broke my peace with Heaven!' &c.

Between the spirit and the earthenware
  That folds its essence in some airy chink,
None know exactly whereabouts,) is quite
  As good a thing :—especially at night.

At all events, a conscience-load of sins
  Is not the thing to go to bed upon :
For, when the work of wickedness begins,
  It very seldom leaves your sleep alone ;
You see the devil sitting on your shins,
  Or wry-faced fiends, that pull you bone from bone,
While, through the curtain, peers—the nursery Thug,—
Old Raw-head's blank, dilapidated mug.

But I had nothing rankling at my breast
  To make me feel uneasy at a vision ;
In fact, if the plain truth must be confessed,
  I'd always held ghost-learning in derision ;
And deemed such dismal theory, at best,
  Propounded by some schoolroom politician,
To frighten naughty children into good :
But, on it came !—It looked like flesh and blood !

She was indeed a bright and lovely maid,
  In the young spring of sweet unsullied youth ;
Her silken hair was carelessly arrayed
  Above a brow that seemed all light and truth ;
And, loosely wreathed amid its golden braid,
  Mingled the myrtle and the rose ; in sooth,
The last might veil its blushes for the glow
Of those delicious cheeks that warmed below !

And O, those lips ! their deep, luxurious hue
  Had kindled up the coldest anchorite ;

And those dear eyes—the softest, loveliest blue
    That ever yet drank in this earthly light,—
And the pure Grecian profile, ever new,
    And ever brightening on the raptured sight,
That hung upon it with untiring love,
It seemed just moulded for the worlds above!

But I describe no more: hand, arms, and feet
    Must all be of your own imagination.
Indulgent reader! can you not complete,
    When these are granted without limitation,
A face and form unutterably sweet,
    Quite worthy of your private adoration?
If not—you must excuse the mild misgiving—
You are the very rummest mortal living!

The garlands floating on her gentle head,
    The light, unstudied negligence of dress,
The music rising at her airy tread,
    The halo of entrancing tenderness
That hung upon her looks, and would have shed
    Its light upon the soul most passionless,
And warmed its dull, phlegmatic chords to fire,
Proclaimed alike THE GENIUS OF THE LYRE!

She paused a moment—half irresolute—
    Then, o'er her bright, angelic countenance,
A smile, as quick as the wild stars that shoot
    At midnight through the glittering expanse,
Gleamed; as I lay in gazing wonder mute,
    Like one just waking from an iron trance:
And, lightly tripping to my side, she laid
Her small, soft hand on mine, and laughing, said:—

' Forgotten ?—and so soon !—you used to swear
   That you were mine for ever; but, it seems,
Such vows as yours are but of worthless air,
   False as the mirage of our summer dreams ;
It was not thus when last we wandered where
   Old Trent rolls dimpling in the pale moonbeams !
Are you neglectful—or unkind—or both?
Or don't you know the 'nature of an oath ?'

' Awake—awake !' A sudden thrill went glancing
   Through every vein at those delicious tones :
I jumped, as jump too curious mortals chancing
   Unwittingly to bring their knuckle-bones
Too near a charged electric :—still advancing,
   Laughed the sweet vision at my drowsy groans;
I started up,—and, for that pure embrace,
A martyr might have left his resting-place !

'Twas like a kiss between first cousins, which
   You know is such a licensed salutation,
(Although it seems a sort of moral ditch
   To virgin aunts, and quite a thing that *they* shun—
In pounds and precepts they are always rich),
   It needs no kind of silly affectation ;
In fact, it's quite a case of give and take,
Perhaps a pout,—or, ' Don't, for goodness' sake !'

Just such was ours : and, in the gentle smother
   Attendant on extempore caresses,
No wonder that I started, as another
   Nocturnal visitant, whose silver tresses
And withered forehead might have graced the mother
   Of the young beauty thus exchanging kisses,
Appeared : I'm sure I wished her, in my fury,
A thousand miles below the Petty Cury.

She seemed a matron stately and severe,
   And curiously old : I don't pretend
To tell a lady's age within a year,—
   No pleasing acquisition, in a friend,—
And, in the present case, I almost fear
   To venture on a guess, as, in the end,
You'll find she made some very rash admissions
Concerning divers old geometricians.

Withal, she was a hard, ill-favoured dame,
   And much I wondered what it all portended;
Devoutly wishing, if 'twere quite the same
   To her and hers, the nightly call were ended:—
But, nearer to my bedside still she came,
   And—since we know 'least said is soonest mended,'—
I sat in silence, and in some confusion;
This second visit looked so like intrusion.

The first was well enough; but, really, this
   Had placed the matter quite beyond a joke:
Besides, the owner of the ancient phiz
   Among my ribs commenced a rattling poke
With a sharp crab-stick, which proceeding is
   Enough to madden one, when just awoke!
Twisting at last from one tremendous teaser,
I rolled my (night)-gown round my head—like Cæsar.

Then, casting an exterminating scowl,
   As if to finish what the thrust began,
While glowed the indignation of her soul
   Along her cheek, she grunted,—'Well, young man,
I came, although you seem, upon the whole,
   Quite at your ease without me, just to warn
A simple youth, like you, against the danger
Of listening to that good-for-nothing stranger.

'My name is SCIENCE : and a glorious train
   Are they who, in their age and generation,
Forsook the false, the frivolous and vain,
   To follow me with proper veneration :
I needn't say they quickly found their gain,
   Besides conferring honour on the nation.
You needn't stare so, Mr. What's-your-name,
But run your eye along the rolls of Fame!

'Think of old Euclid!—he was one of mine;
   So was Pythagoras, Eudoxus, Plato :
We've nothing, in these days of love and wine,
   By way of talent, worth a cold potato;
And what we have is wasted at the shrine
   Of that unblushing, idle minx, Erato;
The cause of more than half the plagues that are :
I'm sure I often wish her very far!

'Think of old Archimedes! Aristarchus,—
   Of Nicomedes,—Eratosthenes,—
Lucretius,—Posidonius, and Hipparchus,—
   Of Menelaus, and Sosigenes,—
Of Strabo,—Seneca,—Pliny, and Plutarchus,
   Of Aulus Gellius,—Proclus,—Diocles,—
Poor Ptolemy our gratitude, too, taxes,
Just call to mind his Μεγάλη Σύνταξις.

'There's Leonardo, too, and Roger Bacon,—
   Copernicus, and Tycho,—and we find
My Galileo, who had undertaken
   That hardest task of all—to teach the blind;
A set of drowsy, drivelling priests to waken,
   Who gave, alas! an answer most unkind;
And, pointing to the faggots, fire and post,
Concisely warned him to recant or roast.

'Poor Bruno was less fortunate, and found
   Small favour in each stupid heathen heart;
And soon, alas! a glorious bonfire crowned:
   Then Kepler, Huyghens, Napier, and Des Cartes,
With mighty Newton, trod the golden ground;
   And Franklin,—Euler,—Herschel, played their part!—
A splendid roll-call, as you must acknowledge,
And yet you don't adore your Dons in college.

'You vilify them, sir, as musty wretches,
   A band of bumptious and annoying sinners;
Bound in white neckcloths, and ill-made black breeches,
   And gluttonously lined with venison dinners;
Who bloat like drones upon the college riches,
   And pass their lives in bullying beginners:
I'm doting, perhaps,—life's lamp may want the snuffers,—
Still, I could hug them all,—I could, the dear old buffers!

'But where's the good of raking up the trash
   That youth, and ignorance, and idle spite
Conspire in hurling at pursuits that clash
   With the fulfilment of their vain delight?
It sparkles harmless, like your summer flash
   Around the eminence it cannot smite.
Disdain their follies; fly the recreant throng!
But, above all things, cut the paths of song!

'The din of battle, and her smoking plain,
   Hoof-torn and trampled, are not further set
From the seclusion of my peaceful reign,
   Than is the poet's myrtle coronet:
Fantastic, wild, imaginative, vain,
   To live in folly, and to die in debt,—
This is his golden recompense, who chooses
To turn quill-driver to the gentle Muses!

'Yet have I seen, with tears in these old eyes,
    The midnight wax consume its wasted flame ;
While you, neglectful of the precious prize,
    Of honour's interest, and of duty's claim ;
And all the glory and the gold that lies
    Along the paths of academic fame
While all your friends around were dumb and busy,
Sat worshipping that false and idle hussy !

'Then, once again, forsake her, and a crown
    By these old fingers gathered shall be thine,
More firm and lasting than the light renown
    That pays the love-lorn Poet's hungry whine ;
Fling down the bay-leaf for the cap and gown ;
    Once more—and but once more—I say, "Be mine !"'
She paused :—I answered with a stupid stare ;
I scarce remembered what I was, or where.

The camel flounders in the desert sand ;
    And sinks before Sirocco's murderous flame :
The bird drops powerless by the basilisk scanned ;
    And chloroform makes people strangely tame :
'Tis said one slumbers by a Vampyre fanned :
    If Mesmerism's true, it's much the same ;
And thus we faint and fail, as o'er us flows
The dreary torrent of superfluous prose !

A genuine scold,—no matter how absurd,—
    Must necessarily keep her victim neuter,
Unless you manage to slip in a word ;
    (Which, ten to one, won't puzzle or confute her) ;
Or, as a double-barrel stops a bird,
    You somehow cunningly contrive to shoot her ;
Which,—even if you're handy with a gun,—
Except in savage countries, can't be done.

Were I Sultan and a Despot, thus
    Should run the proclamation of my reign :—
'𝕷ong-winded people must be brought to 𝖀s,
    𝕭y all who favour in 𝕺ur eyes would gain :
𝕬nd, that their cure may cause no needless fuss,
    𝕹or give our 𝕳ead 𝕻hysician work in vain,
𝕺𝕷e do command him to extract their lungs,
𝕿heir jaw-bones dislocate, and split their tongues.'

And, if such remedy should prove too mild,
    I shall proceed to raze their habitations ;
And then to pillory both man and child
    Upon the list of all their near relations,
Who, being very naturally riled,
    Will much discountenance their long orations :
Compressing under salutary locks
The lid of each confounded chatter-box.

Such is my theory :—I didn't follow
    Its obvious bearing, in the present case,
Simply because I rather thought she'd hollo,
    And rather more than thought she'd scratch my face,
If I tried violence ; and, by Apollo,
    My patron saint, great were your bard's disgrace
If sound of strife and scientific squealing
Had only penetrated through my ceiling.

Because above me dwelt the Dean ; and he
    Being, like other Dons, intensely vicious,
And therefore prone in everything to see
    Something, to say the least of it, suspicious,
Would have descended in his *robe-de-nuit*,
    And, probably, considered it judicious
To catch the blooming Genius of the Lyre,
And pitch her, harp and all, behind the fire.

At all events, *her* character and mine
   Would have received a very shocking blow :
I never could have penned another line,
   In fact I couldn't have remained below ;
For Deans assume prerogatives divine,
   And what they say admits no mortal ' No.'
How he'd have snubbed—that monster grave and hairy—
The mild excuse of ' Please, sir, it's a fairy ! '

' I'm sure I heard him tumble out of bed !
   Madam ! for goodness' sake, depart ! ' I cried :
' Hark ! on the stairs I hear his clumsy tread ;
   If you can't vanish, run ma'am—do ! and hide.'
Maddened with fear, a good deal more I said ;
   To which she, rather haughtily, replied,
' Boy, the brief moment of this present vision
Must carry on its wing your last decision ! '

' It shall,' rejoined the Nymph, and o'er the strings
   Her flying fingers to the words gave time ;
And launched each syllable on liquid wings,
   Yet melting all in one harmonious chime :
Oh, if the fairy music that she flings,
   Be marred by hand of mine, forgive the crime !
Remember that my head, and heart, and hands, are
Curbed by the fly-wheel of this stubborn stanza !

    ' It shall, proud Queen, but not for thee,
       Though stores of guerdon-gold be thine!
    The nobler heart shall beat for me,
       Who only call the myrtle mine ;
    The brightest immortality—
       The foremost niche in Glory's line
    Are all for him, and him alone,
       Who worships at the Muse's throne !

' Men call me false, and call me vain,
   Yet little reck the joys that flow
Untasted in my glorious fane,
   Where thousands learn to smile below,
And millions more, that wear the chain
   Of earthly care on breast and brow,
Might sun them at its living fire,
And bless the GENIUS OF THE LYRE!

' But you, ye base mechanic slaves,
   To SCIENCE fettered, heart and limb,
What know ye of the sparkling waves
   On Aganippe's crystal brim,
Or the sweet shadow of her caves,
   Where inspiration falls on him
Whose breast can thrill to higher things
Than ever crossed your visionings?

' The flame that, in the days of yore,
   In free, unclouded splendour shone;
And warmed, on old Achaia's shore,
   The warrior men of Marathon,
May light the wondering earth once more,—
   Once more may call the world its own;—
And, shall he dare forsake my shrine,
Whom I have called, and marked as mine?'

Already, the ripe garlands of renown
   Around my brow their magic lustre shed;
Already I, the Lion of the town,
   Was courted, quoted, praised, caressed, and fed;

Already, I had knocked one Proctor down,
    And set a price upon the Dean's thick head;
When forms and figures changed, and lights, and hues;
    Much in the style of the Dissolving Views.

Just then Dame Science, quivering, passion-pale,
    Sprang forward, like a 'Gætula leæna,'
To seize the startled Nymph: of no avail
    Seemed all my desperate attempts to screen her;
My dizzy brain spun round,—a whirlwind gale
    Of waking thought confounded all I'd seen or
Fancied in sleep,—and then a sad slow knell:
It was,—no,—yes, it *was* the Chapel Bell!

ORIANDE.

EXTRACT INTRODUCTORY.

'In the meanwhile,' rejoined the King of Persia, 'have the goodness to inform me more particularly of the states and people of the sea, upon which subject I am wholly ignorant. I have, indeed, heard of people living in the sea, but I have always considered such relations as mere fables. Nothing, however, appears to be more true, after what you have told me. I have, indeed, a convincing proof in you, who are of marine descent, and are now my wife; an honour such as no other inhabitant of the earth has previously been able to boast of. There is still one thing that seems unaccountable, and of which I beg you to inform me. I cannot comprehend how you are able to live, act, or move in the water, without being drowned. With us, there are but few persons who have the art of remaining under water for more than a few moments; and even these generally perish there, unless they quit it within a certain time, according to their respective ability and strength.'

'Sire,' replied Gulnare, 'I will satisfy your majesty with the greatest pleasure. We are accustomed to walk at the bottom of the sea, in the same manner as you do upon the earth, and are enabled to breathe in the water as others do in the air. Instead, therefore, of our being suffocated, as would be the case with you, the water contributes to our existence. What may seem also very remarkable is, that it does not wet our clothes; and when, therefore, we visit the earth, we are under no necessity of drying them.

'I ought not to neglect telling you that the water does not in the least prevent our seeing, as we can open our eyes in it without sustaining the least inconvenience. And, as our sight is for the most part extremely good, we can, notwithstanding the depth of the sea, perceive objects as clearly in it as others do upon earth. It is the same with us at night. We have the moon to enlighten us, and the planets and stars are not hidden. With respect also to our kingdoms: as the sea is much more spacious than the earth, it affords a greater number, and some of them of greater extent. They are divided into provinces ; and in every province there are a great many well-peopled towns. In short, there is with us an infinity of nations, of different manners and customs, in the same way as upon the earth.

'The palaces of our kings and princes are extremely superb and magnificent. They are formed of marble of different colours ; of rock-crystal, with which the sea abounds ; of mother-of-pearl, coral, and other most valuable materials. I do not mention pearls. The very largest that are seen on earth would be of no estimation among us ; and they are only worn by common people.

'As we have the power of transporting ourselves wherever we wish with incredible velocity, we have no occasion for carriages or equipage. None of our kings, however, are without their stables and studs of marine horses ; but they are, for the most part, only made use of for amusements, or when we have feasts or public rejoicings. Some will take great pains in training them for riding ; and afterwards mount them to show their ability in the race. Others will harness them to cars, made of mother-of-pearl, ornamented with a thousand different sorts of shells, all of the most brilliant colours. I pass over an infinity of other very curious particulars in regard to these marine countries,' added the queen, &c. &c.—BEDER and GIAUHARE, *Arabian Nights.*

CANTO I.

No sound of Earth to break the charm
 That reigns within the Fairy dell ;
The rounded moon shines clear and calm,
 The glassy river owns the spell :
Unripplingly it wanders on,
 Through scathed ravines of limestone gray,
Where never yet the sunlight shone,
 Nor ever blew the gales of day ;
Where sullen trees for ever drink
 The darksome water winding by,
And rugged crags o'erhang the brink,
 Like fossil, old-world Tantali :
They seem to watch the water-weeds
 That sway so idly to and fro ;

Perhaps they count the bubble-beads,
 And wonder why they sail so slow;
Perhaps they're striving to outstare
 Their rough old faces, glassed below;
Perhaps they're very happy there,
 Perhaps they're not—but who's to know?

Ah me! while yet a child at school,
I knew each reach and bend and pool
Of that old stream; we called it then
'The River of the Haunted Glen.'
For many a magic tale was told
Of those deep waters, clear and cold;—
Men said, the boldest swimmer, there,
 Went writhing helpless down to death;
They told us that the very air
 Held something strange to mortal breath;
They said the owls that built aloof
 In those dark trees, knew more than we;
They said their nests were schoolboy-proof—
 We felt that this could scarcely be.
Amid black roots and rocks below,
 They said swam wise and wary fish,
That never rose to mortal throw,
 Nor stretched their length on mortal dish.
Bluff Isaac Walton once, they said,
 Went empty home with surly strides,
And brake his rod and beat his head;
While gaily laughed that river-bed,
 With flicker of their steel-bright sides.

But stranger things than these they told,
 Those quaint old prosy swains;
They said, that pulseless current rolled
 Through the deep Earth's cold veins,

Long mining miles, with wind and turn,
From its far-flooded fountain-urn ;
Beneath strange vaults, for ever bright
With that great river's ghastly light :
And one long labyrinth, broad and high,
Unmeasured yet by mortal eye,
They swore ran seaward, far away—
They knew it well, themselves, for they
Had heard, resounding in those caves,
The tumbling of the Baltic waves.
They said that when the clock struck ten,
Sea-fairies filled the Haunted Glen!

Long years had passed since that young time,
And I had roved in many a clime ;
Through distant lands, o'er foreign seas,
With course as wayward as the breeze.
Much had I learnt, and much forgot,
Ere once again I trod the spot
Which, even in the sternest heart,
Will find and probe some tender part,
And thrust upon the coarsest brain
A pleasure deeply seamed with pain.
For, O how few can calmly stand
Where, launched on life, they left the land,
And think, amid that schoolboy scene,
Of what they were—and might have been!

Unchanged I found the Fairy Glen—
   The stones, and owls, and trees, the same—
Ah! blithe young comrades grown to men—
   How dear to me was every name,
Carved rudely out, with painful skill,
On those grim willows, drinking still!

I sat me down to muse, and feel
   How sweeping and how stern the change ;
To catch old memories by the heel,
   And tell spent years in backward range ;
To dream of those, the loved of yore,
Now scattered all the wide world o'er :
Some herded in the slavish ring
That fawn and whine round Gold, the King,
Some battling on in mart and camp,
Some wrinkling by the midnight lamp,
Some buoyed on Fortune's prosperous flow,
Some grounded on the shoals of woe ;
And one, our darling and our best—
O, who would break his early rest !
Unharmed, unwearied in the strife,
How brief, how bright, *his* glimpse of life !

One dropping sand-grain, so they say,
Will all in shining splinters lay
   Boulogna's crystal bell ;
E'en so, sometimes, a wild-bird's call,
A step, a sound, a leaflet's fall,
   Will startle those who dwell
In the calm halls of memory—
The palace of a reverie—
And shatter all its fretwork fair,
Like frail Alnaschar's basket-ware.
So started I—as up the glen,
So seldom touched by feet of men,
   A hoary stranger came :
With slow staff-measured steps he strode,
A mighty beard of silver snowed
   O'er half his ancient frame ;

His haggard eyes, in darkness bound,
Were sternly fixed upon the ground,
  Nor once confronted mine :
He might have passed, in days of yore,
For sightless palmer from the shore
  Of holy Palestine.

I say not that no secret fear,
As that strange blind old man drew near,
  My better manhood shook.
Some spirit of the lonely glen,
Or stern Enchanter—in whose den
Caged virgins weep, and harmless men,
  Lured from the pipe and crook—
He seemed, and all my fond old nurse
On windy nights would oft rehearse,
Of people that grew worse and worse,
And never said a bible-verse,
  And died in hideous pain ;
Yet in their graves would not lie flat,
But started at the sexton's pat,
Exclaiming, 'What the devil's that?'
  Rose freshly in my brain.
How, marked for endless penance-doom,
Instead of resting in the tomb,
They nightly stalked through wind and gloom
  And frost and showering snow ;
Till, down the roaring chimney-shaft,
In rage and spite they shrieked and laughed,
Detecting, with infernal craft,
  The bad boy couched below !

Her aim was good, her means were ill,
She quacked us with a dangerous pill,

For, to this very day,
Pale 'Bogey' sniggling round the door—
Or 'Raw-head's' visage, cracked and sore—
I know quite well would make me roar
In the most rueful way:
And thus, as towards my lonely seat
The figure came with noiseless feet,
My heart as hard as Hamlet's beat,
'Till, desperately brave at last,
I gave 'good morrow' as it passed.

Slowly, sadly, paused the blind,
And made me answer, calm and kind;
He was not used to speak, he said:—
He thought that all mankind were dead:
He seldom met them in his walk;
Or, if he did, they wouldn't talk,
But scampered home, as if they feared
The very waving of his beard!

'Good gracious, sir, you can't mean that!'
Cried I; 'we're all alive and kicking!
You shouldn't walk so like a cat,
Your steps down this lone pathway picking.
It frightens people, don't you see?
I'll take my oath it startled me.
What means this hermit-solitude?
Comes it of evil or of good?
What from the common world doth bar you?—
If bar it doth—in short, who are you?'

With calm, commanding sign,
These random words of mine

The old man checked, and sat him down,
Where the sunburnt moss grew thick and brown
　　On the trunk of a fallen oak.
' If thou wouldst learn,' he sternly said,
' Why this rough dale I blindly tread,
　　And bear the bitterest yoke
That ever crushed with slavish load
A wretch upon life's thorny road,
Hopeless alike of help or grace,
Bear with me for a little space.

' I am not of this present age—
　　Three hundred years have dreamed away
Since upon life's ungrateful stage
　　I fretted *my* short hour away;
I have no share in earth or sky—
　　That is over—past and done.
Listen, and I'll tell thee why
　　I stand again below the sun.

' I bore—but O, how long ago!—
　　The blazon of a knightly shield;
Knew how to give and take a blow,
　　And fought in many a famous field.
Right well could I recall the tale
Of days when I wore shirt of mail;
Of grand old battles, where the slain
Lay thick as daisies on the plain;
Of tilts where neither champion cried
' Enough,'—till in the lists he died!
But let it pass, for never more
Shall youth's hot blood these limbs restore,
And ne'er again where vanguards meet
Shall dash my old bay charger's feet,

Yet still, sometimes, in waking dreams,
Through flying smoke the armour gleams ;—
Resounds again the anvil-clash
   Of blades upon the targe ;
Again the driven lances flash
   Along the line of charge ;
And whistling high across the sky the iron hailstorm comes,
Drowned in the crash of trumpets and the clattering of the drums !

'I loved of course, for who did not,
To whom was given the blissful lot
   To live in times like those ?
The sweet young Lady Violet—
Her image haunts my darkness yet—
   Threw my first tournay-rose !
A locket of her sunbright hair
   Lay warm upon my breast ;
Her tiny glove 'twas mine to wear
   Amid my horse-tail crest.
Her father was an English earl,
But a dull bigot and a churl ;
He loved me not, and, worst of all,
He warned me from his castle hall ;
Nay, more, he bade, in heathen spite,
His chaplains curse me day and night !
Little I recked of curses then,
But curse they did, those bat-faced men !

'At last, when failed their drawling ban,
He tried a much more likely plan,
And bribed a blackguard musketeer
   To shoot me from behind a hedge—

Would I had caught the rascal near,
   He should have felt a broadsword's edge—
" A pound to hit him in the head,
A purse of pounds to shoot him dead!"
Such were the standing orders—yet
I courted Lady Violet.

' One night—one happy night in June—
   I met her at the garden-gate,
And, by the friendly lantern-moon,
   I deeply swore that never Fate
Should tempt me from one dear design,
Or thwart me till I called her mine!
The south wind through the garden sprang,
   And shook the blooming chestnut-cones,
But mournfully methought it sang,
As if it had ridden where church-bells clang,
   And caught their funeral tones.
Like whispers of that secret ear,
   Whose night-voice is so clear and low :
O, pray for those that helpless hear
   The footfall of a coming woe!

' Away, away, I rode full spur!—
I always rode madly when thinking of her—
The parting sign was fondly flung,
As down the slopes bay Norman sprung;
At hoof-stroke, snort, and fiery bound,
The living echoes danced around,
As gleamed on yonder mountain gray
The first grave smile of rising day.

' Sudden and loud my courser neighed,
His eager ears are backward laid,

His raven mane is backwards thrown,
For the echoes that follow are not of his own!
  And, fleet as the light,
  On a steed milk-white,
 A fairy form shot by;
  She gave me no heed,
  But patted her steed,
 And rode as the bird would fly.

' O, bled my horse's flanks I ween,
As I dashed him after her over the green!
For her face—oh, Heaven!—her face was one
To see and to die!—for like it was none;
O, I would have given my hopes of grace
For another look at that sweet young face!
Poor bay Norman suffered for her—
Madly I smote him with fist and with spur—
His breath with fluttering sobs he drew,
But his heart was good and his mettle was true,
And when he was failing I lifted him through,
For I knew we were close to the edge of the glen,
And, ride as she might, I must ride with her then!

' Paused her fiery palfrey white,
Upon the crest of yonder height,
As, drenched with sweat and splashed with blood,
Beside her my brave charger stood,
With stiff-stretched neck and trembling limb,
Staring blindly over the brim.

' Unheeding of my horse's tread,
She sat nor turned her queenly head,
But gazed with longing wistful eyes
Full on the purpling eastern skies.

The fingers of one slender hand
Played on her sparkling bridle-band,
The other smoothed her golden hair,
Blown rudely by the morning air.
O, tell me not of right or wrong,
For hearts are weak and passion strong,
And, in a moment, lapse and fall
May wreck the firmest heart of all !
The sudden pulse that shook my frame—
It was not blood, but blasting flame !
The thrill that shot from spur to glove —
O, it was madness more than love !
Ay, spurn me—mock me if thou wilt—
I know my folly, feel my guilt;
But calm yon aspen's trembling branch,
Cry, halt ! where leaps the avalanche,
And then, and not till then, reclaim
The love-struck wretch with Reason's name !
She looked, she need have done no more—
She smiled—she spoke—and all was o'er.

' " Who is the warrior locked in steel
   That rides by the light of the moon ?
     What would he with me,
      The Queen of the Sea ?
   Let him but name the boon.
For yonder, down in the lamp-lit glen,
Are gathered together my fairy-men ;
I'm riding to find for them something to do.
Warrior, say, shall they work for you ?"

' I looked, and lo ! far down the glen
Swarmed the delicate fairy-men,

Coming and going with lamps and bells,
To the musical chime of the trumpeter-shells.
Some were linked in a twinkling ring,
And danced whenever they found a spring;
Some sat high on the lonely rocks,
Twisting water-weed into their locks;
Some were at play in the moon-lit stream;
Some were plaiting her silver beam;
Some were making the wild-cat growl;
Or picking up pebbles to fling at an owl;
Others were playing at "Who'll catch me?"
Or cutting their names on the rind of a tree.

'" Now, by Saint George!" I wildly cried,
"To live in thy smiles and to ride by thy side
For one short hour were joy divine—
What would it be could I call thee mine?
  Ah! Queen of the Sea,
   Cannot it be?
Don't say no, for it's little to me
What those nice nimble sprites can do:
I can't think of them for looking at you."

'" And, warrior, wouldst thou dare with me
To pass down under the vaulted sea?
And wouldst thou thus for aye resign
The light of the sun that never may shine
On eyes that ever have seen the things
That girdle the shrine of the salt sea springs?
If not, beware of oaths misplaced,
And,—don't be taking me round the waist!

'" But, if thy heart be bold and true,
 And thou wouldst pass with me,

The charm is mine to carry thee through
　　The barriers of the sea.

'"The coy and bashful maids of earth
　　Hang backward every one,
And hold the love of slender worth
　　That's lightly lost and won.

'"No sickly shame is known with us,
　　No flattering falsehood ours,
Whose hearts are free, as leaps the sea
　　Around our crystal towers.

　'"But swear to me first,
　　That thy bosom hath nursed
No love of a mortal maid;
　　That no vow hath been spoken
　　That may not be broken—
Swear boldly, on thy blade!
Or else my charm shall shield thee not
Beneath old Ocean's furthest grot;
Though thou shouldst hide thee deeper there
　　Than spins the mariner's lead,
Where the great serpents writhe and glare,
　　And our boldest fear to tread;
Where Etna strikes her fiery fangs
　　A thousand miles below;
Where foul Charybdis froths and clangs,
　　And wrecks wash to and fro;
Or screen thee in the darkest ice
　　Where polar midnights frown;
Ay, there, with hot and hungry eyes
　　Should Vengeance hunt thee down!
Ties like these we may not sever,
And a broken oath can be mended never."

'O! mad and fatal hour—I swore,
  Ay, swore by knightly belt and spur,
That I had never loved before,
  Nor pledged the hand I gave to her!
Ah! Violet—sweet Violet!
  If in their graves the dead can hear,
Forgive me—pity and forget
  The sightless outcast mourning here!
The wretch that sapped thy beauty's bloom,
The wretch that hurled thee to the tomb,
The wretch that dared thy love to slight—
The perjured fiend—the recreant knight!

'I swore. She snatched my willing hand,
  And flung the gauntlet on the grass:
" As dies the foam-flake on the sand,
  Earthly leaven part and pass!
Warrior, by the charm of power,
Strongest in this moonlight hour,
That hath yet the grasp of mortals
    Ever defied;
At whose voice the great sea-portals
    Trembling divide;
By the spell that all obey
    Under the sea,
Hold within thy breast of clay
    Life such as we!
Take the breath and take the blood
Of the children of the flood:
Taking, plight thee, heart and hand,
To me, the Lady Oriande!

'" 'Tis done! the sluggish gales of earth
  Are life no more to thee,

Thy world is now the ocean's girth,
    Thine element the sea !
And, lo ! the moon begins to pale,
My men are clamorous in the dale.
Beyond our gates, by day or night,
They cannot live but in her light ;
Were but a cloud to cross the sky,
Many would faint, and some would die ;
Now the morning breaks indeed,
So mount thee on my fairy steed !"

' No time was then to pause or think,—
    Behind the bright Sea Queen
I sprang, and plunging o'er the brink,
    We lit in the deep ravine.
Such a flight, and such a fall,
Had shivered steed of earthly stall
Into as many million bits
As when the roaring bomb-shell splits.
Such a leap, from such a crag,
Had shamed the black-browed Indian's nag,
That once at Shiraz—if, in sooth,
Arabian legends hold the truth—
Alive with clockwork soared away
With Prince Firouz on New-year's day ;
For light as gossamer we fell,
And landed scatheless in the dell.

' Then all from up and down the glen
Ran the dutiful fairy-men ;
Such joy was theirs their Queen to see,
Scarcely one of them looked at me ;
For each had a wreath or a daisy-chain,
To hang about her palfrey's mane.

Poor little fellows, they valued more
The silliest flower that blooms ashore,
Than heaped sea-wealth, and in their eyes
Thistle and river-flag waved a prize,
And daisies each a twinkling gem,
Fit for their Queen's own diadem!

'From the far stables of the sea
Another steed they led for me—
A spotless filly, white as milk,
With tail and mane like amber silk;
And loud and long with joy they cried
When they beheld me vault astride.
In curious crowds they pressed around;
And how they prattled when they found
That I was all from shot and stab
Shelled and guarded, like a crab!
Yet more, far more than all the rest,
They wondered at my horse-tail crest;
At every nod they laughed again,
Till the owls answered from the glen;
But when, in sport, I drew my sword,
They gave me up and fairly roared.

'Then cried their Queen, "The night is past,
　The orient lights are breaking;
Stars and moon are paling fast,
　And the sons of men are waking.
The fresh south-wind of morning tells;
　Their hymn the birds begin;
My children, sound upon your shells,
　To call the stragglers in!"

'To every crag and cleft around
Warbling bugles tossed the sound;

From crag and cleft and woods and wave
A hundred voices answer gave,
For some were lost the trees among;
And some had climbed the cliffs and hung
On juts and points, like samphire-men,
And durst not clamber down again;
And some, alas! that in their glee
Had gone birds'-nesting up a tree,
Gave answer none, for then and there
Detected in the act they were,
Their little hands yolk-dabbled all,
Their pockets crammed with fledglings small,
And straightway, spite of sobs and howls,
Lynched by the grave, offended owls.

' A low-browed cavern's massive arch
Slowly gorged our swarming march;
Far down its throat as eyes could see
Thronged the small people of the sea,
Each with his tiny lamp held high—
Midmost Oriande and I.
At first our horses scarce could pass,
So rankly shot the mildewed grass,
So close the ribs of trickling stone,
So low the roof and fossil-grown.

' But soon the span grew high and wide,
Glistened the walls on either side;
Beneath us the expanding floor
Lay carpeted with shells and ore;
The rising dome at every turn
More gloriously began to burn;
Deep-set jewels felt the light—
Armories of stalactite

Challenged as the lamps went by;
Flashed the ruby's crimson eye,
Opal and amethyst caught fire,
Like frosty gems in midnight's tiar,
Till all ray-tangled, warp and woof,
One hollow glory blazed the roof.

' And then before us, vast and dim,
   Loomed the great gates of Earth and Sea;
Half-lighted burnt their brazen rim
   With sliding gleams as on came we.
Giants of brass, that bar the way
From this warm world and light of day,
To those calm valleys fathomless,
Above whose dreamy loveliness
The purple waves for ever sweep,
Still floats the great eternal deep.

' Unearthly were the hands, I ween,
That cast and carved that ponderous screen;
Embodyings of no mortal thought
The signs upon those portals wrought.
Such gates perchance were those of old,
If rightly be the story told,
Fashioned by Merlin's weary slaves
In Dynevor's volcanic caves,
When furnace-fires brake nightly out,
And nightly rang the clank and shout,
As fiend-swung hammers rose and fell
To fence Cairmardin citadel.
But what the symbol's burning mould,
And what the winding scroll-work told,
And what the words that must be said
Ere you should see those doors unwed,

Are secrets dear as those which break
Through dying lips for conscience sake.

'But now before us filed aside,
Behold the foremost ranks divide,
On either hand their lamps they swing,
On either hand their bells they ring,
On either hand their throats they strain
Till the red cavern shakes again;
And, as we ride their lines between,
Shout welcome to their matchless Queen!

' "Fling backward the gates of the Sea!
   Our glorious Queen draws near;
Steel-clad warrior! fearless be
   With her to enter here.
      Fling backward the gates of the Sea!

' "The trees and the wind and the moon,
   Right wonderful things are they,
But better breathe *we* in the pearly noon
   Of our ocean's boundless day!
      Fling backward the gates of the Sea!

' "The lamps of the bridal are lit—
   The bride and her bridegroom are here—
Their hot steeds eagerly champ the bit
   Until the path be clear!
      Fling backward the gates of the Sea!"'

Thus far the legend, vaguely told
  With bitter jest and lightless mirth ;
Such as are theirs who tales unfold,
  They fain would hide from Heaven and earth,
Yet cannot stifle, conscience-wrung,
The babbling fiend that goads the tongue.
Brief was the silence ere again
Resumed the patriarch of the glen.

CANTO II.

' O! man, thou tyrant of the patient land,
　　Where all is thine, to carve—to change—to reap!
For whom the elements toil hand in hand,
　　For whom the numbered planets nightly sweep;
Come down with me upon the frontier sand,
　　And gaze upon the calm, imperial deep!
Teach me his wonders—thou whose daring eyes
Unravel all the secret of the skies!

' Count me the Kingdoms of that guarded world!
　　They laugh to scorn thy prying and thy pains!
Kingdoms whose map was never yet unfurled;
　　Kingdoms thrice wider than thy swarthy plains;
Kingdoms from whence, in every storm upwhirled,
　　Leaps a new spark of wonder! what remains?
What waste unhoped-for wealth, what realms of spoil,
They vaunted power and skill to tempt—and foil!

' He bears thy ships, but not as bears the slave:
　　He is thy friend, or foe:—he fears thee not.
Beneath his blue unfathomable wave,
　　Thou art not monarch of one inch-wide plot:
He yields thee nothing—save a boundless grave,
　　Where the gray bones of myriads blanch forgot,
Till Earth's thick tombs and Ocean's changeless bed
Alike shall render up their trust of dead.

　' But now return with me to pass
　Those twin stupendous gates of brass,
　That never yet their cumbrous pride
　To mortal man had wheeled aside.

A hundred hands each portal swung,
The brazen axles groaned and rung,
In stately strength invincible,
To all but that commanding spell:
Until at last, as in the Spring,
When woodsman hatchets glance and ring,
Before the biting, hateful axe
Some forest-monarch nods and cracks,
Till, downward, with a sudden roar,
Crashing he goes, to bloom no more,
So, backward hurled with furious clang,
Those everlasting barriers rang,
  And, trembling in the gap,
Blue endless lengths of landscape haze
Burst on my blank astounded gaze,
Fanned with such breath as lingering strays,
Towards the calm death of rosy days,
  O'er Spring's own violet lap!

'But, on—press on! with clattering feet
The marble path our palfreys beat;
The clashing doors behind us close,
But lovelier yet the picture glows,
And fresher still the breezes sweep,
And madlier still my pulses leap!
What care I for the world above,
Or wealth, or life, or woman's love;
With that fair thing beside me riding,
  With that rich dream around me cast—
Behind, those gallant gates dividing
  THIS, from the tame unworthy past!

'She whispered much—those regal eyes
  Down-shining on her horse's mane,

But I was gazing on the skies,
  And answered scarce a word again.

' Even as when some lover greets,
  In the long twilight garden-walk,
A promised bride—his bosom beats,
  He clasps her hand and hears her talk:

' And yet an idle answer gives,
  In broken phrase at random shot,
While she, within whose glance he lives,
  In that full joy seems all forgot.

' So I, from whose irresolute breast
  One smile of hers all else had driven,
Scarce heeded though by lips addressed,
  For which the world I just had given.

' Well might my senses yield in truth,
  Amid a scene so strange ;
Well might the pulses of my youth
  Leap at each magic change !
Each wonder of the ocean-sky,
That over all hung bright and high,
A living sphere shot through and through,
With changing rays of gorgeous hue,
Now rosy pink—now richly blue—
Now, all its colours fused anew,
  A dome of emerald glass ;
Whilst ever through the vaulted height
Sheet-lightning gleams broke thick and bright,
Quick as athwart some August night
  The fire-fly meteors pass !

'And see, within its round expanse,
What myriad beings dart and glance
Far, far above our upturned eyes,
They poise, and wheel, and swoop, and rise,
Some sheathed in mail—some soaring dark,
Some every scale a golden spark—
A hundred hands point out the shark,
   Apollyon of the sea !
There sweeps the dolphin's radiant pride,
And there the bold sea-swordsmen ride,
And there the clouded mackerel glide
   In some dusk mountain's lee.
They flit among the coral-woods
   That, half-way up the sky,
So calmly toss their jewelled hoods
   As the slow tide sweeps by :
Some that hoar-sparkling branch and blow,
Like ancient forests bowed with snow,
Some drenched with such sweet rosy glow
   As floods the hawthorn spray,
When sap of April's fairy blood
Stirs warm within the small red bud,
And lights a thousand stars to stud
   The garland of a day !
Around each knotted mountain-base
   Trail flowers of tender bloom ;
Their loving tendrils link and lace,
Each breathing in a sister's face
   Her amorous perfume ;
Some clinging to the wet rock's edge,
Some clambering up a dizzy ledge,
Some deepening with a golden hedge
   A cavern's lonely gloom.
And sunny shells glide everywhere,

Along the carpet-sand!
O, Sea, if half thy wonders were
But known to men of upper air,
With me amid thy valleys fair
    How gladly would they stand!

'But, on—press on! before us burn
    The deep sea's purple towers;
The crowd that wait their Queen's return
    Have strewn our path with flowers.
With radiant eyes they meet us,
    As we ride the archway through;
With ringing cheers they greet us,
    From loyal hearts and true:
You might have heard a league away
    The shouting in the squares,
That told of our dismounting
    Before the palace stairs.

'And now within the pillared hall,
    Behold the wedding banquet set;
Ten thousand merry elvesmen small
    Around the glittering tables met;
The Ocean Queen and I alone,
Apart upon our ample throne,
    Beneath a tented canopy,
    Heavy with gorgeous blazonry
And jewels from the central zone.

'How bright she looked! oh, how I hung
On the low music of her tongue!
How fiercely, whispering at her side,
Ran love's tumultuous drowning tide!

What words were mine I know not now,
What fond renewal, vow on vow,
Of one sweet oath—what eager claim
To hear those lips repeat my name!
No matter—be it prose or rhyme,
In every age, in every clime,
A lover's talk is much the same.

' With jovial sound
    The bowls went round
  Beneath us at the board,
Till many a little graceless rogue
Lay chattering out a tipsy brogue,
    Or slumbered fairly floored.
No doubt their Queen was wearied well
With so much courting at a spell,
    For, beckoning to her side
An ancient harper of the Sea,
    She bade him sound, with all his pride,
A song wherein no love should be.

' Strange was his mien, that reverend seer's,
Along whose brow uncounted years
    Had strewn their tribute snow.
Some said that in his awful brain
Futurity lay clear and plain,
    Mapped out for joy or woe:
But all were sure that, since his birth,
He knew the changes of the earth,
    The mysteries of the deep;
Had heard, while yet in manhood's noon,
The waste volcanos of the moon
    Thunder themselves to sleep.
With square and compass could he trace

Each blasting comet's whirlwind race,
    And measure out the year
To each revolving planet-star,
From the broad sun's last furnace-bar
    To Saturn's belted sphere.
He loved to sing the ways of men,
    Their deeds and dreams—as we
Still chronicle with dreary pen
    Dry legends of the sea.
The glittering harp-strings boldly rang,
And thus old Ocean's Nestor sang :—

The Islands of the Blest.

Isles of the blest! what visions bright,
    Were his who, glorious hopes divining,
Sang first of a far fairy-light
    Along the dusk Atlantic shining!

Of Isles from earth far-parted
    By the rolling barrier-wave,
Where the generous and true-hearted
    Live on beyond the grave ;

Where the sage may rest from dreaming,
    And the warrior rest from strife,
And the rich man rest from scheming,
    And the poor man rest from life !

When the wind was blowing gaily,
    And the waves were bursting free,

Around the shining islands
  Of the blue Atlantic sea,
O, many a time, rock-seated,
  Have I with harp in hand
Struck up a jolly roundelay
  To greet that happy band,
Till down came half Elysium
  To dance upon the sand :
And godlike men and heroes
  Went by with prouder tread,
To hear me sing how gratefully
  The living love the dead :
How fathers take their little ones
  To touch the patriot's urn,—
To cry and tremble as they ask,
  'But when will he return?—
The man that was so good to us,
  O, father, where is he?'
'My children, blessed for ever,
  Far, far beyond the sea !
Not the gods that live in heaven,
  To whom our eyes we turn,—
When all the world is praising them,
  And all their altars burn,
Are blest as he whose ashes lie
  So still in yonder urn.
Then think of him, my children,
  And ask him day and night,
To speed you in the forum
  And guard you in the fight ;
And hold this truth for ever,
  When Death has knocked for me,
True heirs are they of Freedom
  Who are fathers of the free !'

But hark! what awful whisper
    Comes hovering o'er the sea,
That echoes up the mountains
    And booms along the lea?
The whirling dance is broken
    And the laughter heard no more,
And not a word is spoken
    As they gather on the shore.

The first who hear that summons—
    I know their faces well—
As those who down in Marathon
    So sternly fought and fell;
When all the Great King's army
    Came down to chain the free;
And Europe stood with Asia,
    Face to face beside the sea.

That wild September sunrise!
    The doom of kings unborn
Hung balanced in thy stormy light,
    Thou memorable morn!
Those endless hordes descending!
    E'en now I see them sweep
Down where the ranks of Athens
    Their own free causeway keep!
In vain, with dust and thunder,
    Each fiery charge is rolled,
Stout hearts are in those kneeling squares,
    Strong shepherds keep the fold;
On the firm fence of lances
    The battle beats in vain,
Though Khorassan's wild horsemen
    Come down with flying rein,

Though fierce Caucasian clansmen
   Their ponderous maces ply,
And sheaves of Indian arrows
   Drive whistling through the sky!

And now the scales are turning—
   'No longer stand at bay!
Up, eager sons of Athens!
   Platæans, clear the way!
Charge where they launch the galleys!
   Charge! Fire them on the shore!
The slaves of King Darius
   Shall see his face no more!'

Thus fell these hero conquerors,
   That pass before me now;
'Twas thus they won the laurel
   That blooms on every brow,
'Twas thus they won the noble praise
   That men shall still repeat,
Whilst yet Macaria's fountain plays
   And freeborn pulses beat,
With hymns in every temple
   And songs at every feast,
'They kept the Gates of Europe
   Against the slavish East!'

Hush! hoarser grows the whisper
   That booms along the shore—
They know the furious music
   Of a battle's distant roar.
Half-heard, the well-known war-cry
   Of Persia sweeps the main,
And, maddening at the sound, they ask,
   'Can we have died in vain?

Can once again the Tyrant
  Have swooped when we are gone,
And all the land be crying
  For us to lead them on?
No, no! our sons are fighting
  To-day in yonder field;
Our names will be their watchword,
  Our sons will never yield!'

Slow falls the roar of battle
  Along the listening sea:
Now who shall tell these conquerors
  If still their Greece be free?
Lo! specked in the blue distance,
  Whilst every heart is dumb
With sick and painful hoping,
  The phantom galleys come:
The ships that on the battle-eve
  Bear home the glorious dead,
Who for their own dear father-land
  Their blood have bravely shed.

The eyes of good Callimachus
  Have caught the signal first,
And, O! the shout of thunder
  That up the blue sky burst!

Their hands are waving Victory!
  Aloft their standards fly!
Hark! they are shouting 'SALAMIS!'
  Shout, brethren, in reply!
And spread the mighty festival,
  And tear the myrtle down,
That each true patriot yonder
  May wear the deathless crown!'

Such, Queen of the deep ocean,
  Was the vision seen by me,
Amid the shining islands
  Of the blue Atlantic sea.

'From song and glare, and lamps and wine,
  We passed. A stately platform-way,
With solemn urns and marble kings;
That ruled of old the salt-sea springs,
  In deep red calm of evening lay—
And she was there, and she was mine!

'From his cold granite pedestal,
There was no statue of them all
But on us looked with awful eyes,
And from the crimson ocean-skies
Caught shade and light alternately,
We almost heard them breathe and sigh.

'Gently she spoke: " The deed is done
That shuts thee out from earth and sun,
And thou hast dared, for love of me,
To pass down under the vaulted sea.

' "I said our hearts were fearless here,
  I thought so till to-day,
But the coyest girl on earth might sneer,
  To see me now repay
So coldly and so bashfully,
What thou hast done so gallantly.
I know not why. From pole to pole
The torn white waters race and roll;

From ice to ice the depths are mine,
As princess of my father's line,
With sand, and shells, and rocks, and flowers,
And vassal elves and marble towers.
Why should I fear lest thou shouldst be
Less happy and less blest than we?

' " For us, the Children of the Foam,
We love our boundless ocean-home;
Seldom we pass the midway pales,
That bar from earth our fairy-dales,
Nor care to ask what joys are theirs,
Self-styled Creation's foremost heirs.

' " And yet we feel that prouder claims,
And wiser thoughts, and loftier aims,
And clearer views, and mightier powers,
May make their lot more blest than ours;
And half I fear, lest when the gloss
  Of this new scene hath worn away,
That thou shouldst only count the loss,
  And hate the doom that bids thee stay,
And spurn the lightly-given hand
Of the unhappy Oriande!

' " Yet blame her not: it is not here,
Within the round sea's vaulted sphere,
Grand though it be, this ardent breast
Could slumber on the shelves of rest.
No—something told and tells me still,
My heart hath yet to drink its fill
Of soul-springs deep with hope and love,
And high thoughts only felt above!
For this I pant, and, day by day,
Thirst vainly for the kindling ray

That yet may teach me how to feel,
For what to wish—to whom to kneel;
To be as those to whom 'tis given,
To bear on earth a soul from Heaven.!
That were a prize . . . and, it is told,
The love of one of mortal mould
May raise us in the golden scale;[1]
And I would rise: the very gale
That kissed me in its morning race,
And blew my hair about my face,
Vexed me with whispers: yes, it said
Even they are better who are dead
Than thus as I, and down the glen,
Went buoyant with the souls of men.
Whom have I here to whom this heart
Aught of its burden may impart?
Who that can hope or strive with me,
Or frame one wish beyond the sea,
Or dare assert that Ocean's birth
May peer with men that walk the earth—
Formed by the self-same hand as they—
Find out the path and force the way?
Not one! their hearts are loyal all,
Who shout within yon crystal hall;
I love them well—and there we end—
I have no hope—no faith—no friend!"

' " By every Saint, sweet Oriande,"
 I said; " By earth no more my own,
I would not yield this dear young hand,
 To lounge upon an Indian throne!

---

[1] 'Now the race to which I belong, have no other means of obtaining a soul, than by forming with an individual of your own the most intimate union of love. I am now possessed of a soul. . . .'—UNDINE.

Talk not of loss to one whose trade
Was only wrought by lance and blade,
Heir to no costlier heritage
Than on a die's cast might one gage,
And laugh to lose: without one tie
To curb his rash knight-errantry.

'"The sage upon his turret-height
Scans the slow changes of the night,
And, stripped of all his darling stars,
Would quickly grin through Bedlam-bars;—
The schoolman o'er the dusty page,
Lashes his flanks in critic rage—
The alchemist, with bootless toil,
Hears only his alembic boil—
The lawyer cares but for his fee,
The merchant but for ships at sea:
Rob them of these and they are lost,
Their life's one aim for ever crossed!
But *I* was trained a soldier rough,
Nor ever yet knew change enough!
I, to whose life as breath and food
Comes wild adventure's wildest mood,
Should I repent me of a deed,
 Which to have done there's not a knight,
But would have given both lance and steed,
 Ay, casque and spurs, with all delight?
No, Oriande, 'tis early yet
To talk of losses or regret."

'Brightly she smiled, her sweet face lit
 With one rich glow of trust and love:
And now beside us glancing flit,
 In shadow of the towers above,

Young nymphs who come their Queen to claim,
And half in sport and half in shame,
Hint slyly at the Love-god's flame.
Ask me no more—a dizzy mist
Hides all, if aught indeed I wist,
Till they restored her bashful charms,
To a delighted bridegroom's arms!

CANTO III.

'What hope is theirs who snatch with lawless clutch
  That Proteus, pleasure, and that phantom, gain?
Who deem that, Life being shortened over-much,
  'Tis wise to jog along with a loose rein?
Alas, their hands but poison all they touch,
  Till the roused Fates, that never wake in vain,
Plunge from their awful eyrie, torch in claw,
Shreeves of the grand Eumenidean law!

'What hope is theirs who, when they gain their end,
  In gathered mantle-fold dare stand elate;
Disdain beneath eternal rules to bend,
  And boldly draw the sword, and fence with Fate?
Who hug the dangerous prize—their deeds defend,
  And answer the accuser hate for hate?
Brave worms that blindly rearing in the dust,
The stern revolving wheel would backward thrust!'

Vague words like these—half muttered, half suppressed,
  Broke thro' the bearded lips of that gray sire;
And then a great sigh shook his aged breast,
  And his blind eyes burnt each a point of fire,
And, as the red sun fell along the west,
  Flooding with crimson light each flinty spire,
And the first owl whooped from the darkening tree,
Urged once again the wonders of the sea.

   'Glorious days that, gone for ever,
      Haunt me still with lingering light,
   Like those airy scenes that fever
      Dreaming brains with vain delight—

Scenes that we would cling to, waking,
  That we loose with passionate pain
When we find the dull day breaking
  Up the cold white window pane!—
Glorious days, along whose track
The wretched night rides doubly black,
Days no more for me that shine,
Let me feel ye once were mine!

' Vain the wish! for firm and fast,
  Fenced and locked and doubly barred,
Stand the gates that o'er the Past—
  Trodden once—keep ruthless guard.

' Memory peeps through chink and joint,
  Sees the steep way wind and turn,
All the guide-boards one way point :—
  'Forward,' still their legend stern.

' None go back, and last night's halt
  Is as far from us to-day,
As is the rim of the blue sky-vault
  Beyond the sun's last fainting ray.

' So be it then : and let me seem
But as a child that tells its dream,
Or crazy graybeard, cracked with age,
Drivelling of manhood's lusty rage,
Firm on his audience to inflict
What none believe—or contradict.

' I envy such, whose draught of bliss
  So graciously withdrawn,
Just leaves uncloyed the goblet's kiss,
  Without the racks of morn.

P 2

But I that curse and grind my teeth
  To think of days gone by,—
Can Heaven above or earth beneath
  Find rest for such as I?

' Far from the giddy throng 'twas ours
To haunt alone the waving bowers;
To wander on through lanes of shade,
Where the red forest rolled and swayed,
Showering its leaves; or idly pause
Beneath some cavern's flinty jaws;
And lingering there, alone with love,
Talk of the crowded world above.

' I see her still, as at my feet
She used to sit with look so sweet;
Her small hands clasped about my knee,
Her thoughtful blue eyes fixed on me,—
Till in their very innocence,
They grew a weight on every sense,
Striking through mine: I never knew
Till hers I saw, what eyes could do!

' Then would she ask, with childlike glee,
For news of Earth beyond the sea;
Yes, news of every kind and sort,
And if we had a Queen at Court?
And how she looked, and how she dressed,
And if she always praised the best?

' Alas! she wondered—well she might—
To find so little in a knight.
"What! carve at meals, and dance in hall,
And ride in armour, men to maul,"
She said ; " why this can scarce be all?

A goodly life!—O, surely they
Who bask amid the smiles of day,
And bear a soul in every breast,
Know more than we:—you only jest.
But ah, I too," she blushing cried,
Her downcast eyes half turned aside,
" Have now a soul, oh, boundless prize!
Tell me of prayers that reach the skies:
Teach me—for this at least you know—
How best one's thanks to Heaven may go;
What least provokes its angry frown,
And calls the kindest answer down!"

'" Alas!" I said, " our priests themselves
Keep mouldy books on mouldier shelves,
Which—so they say—much lore contain,
And might—God knows—make all things plain.
And yet I'm certain in my heart,
There isn't one who knows his part;
But what they *do* you'd scarce believe,—
I only know, last Christmas eve,
They tied our parson to a stick,
And burnt him for a heretic.
Some say that better times are come,
And that a book that's long been dumb
Speaks peace to all;—I hope 'tis true,
I'd roast no mortal—save a Jew.
But whilst our loose church-weathercock
Veers only to mislead the flock,
A man's a fool to risk his hide,
And so my creed's grown rather wide!"
" Can men," she murmured, " be so mad?
O, this is very strange and sad."

'Yet think not that such idlesse light
Alone beguiled time's easy flight.
No, right and left our path lay free,
Through all the labyrinths of the sea.
Now, with a band of hardy elves,
I scaled the savage mountain-shelves;
And up, and up, and up, we clomb,
To hear the breakers howl and foam,
And the desolate storm-wind shriek and yell
To the slow sad clang of the light-house bell.

'Now northward wandering rose we where
No life-sound stirs in the darkling air,
But crouched upon his Arctic throne,
Death holds his midnight court, alone.
There spreads the plain of the printless snow,
Just as it fell, long ages ago;
And the shivering frost-fires wave and stream,
And the ice-crags laugh in their ghastly gleam,
And venturous mariners' teeth, 'tis told,
Come chattering out of their gums with cold,
And faces are shrivelled like apples in May,
And frost-bitten fingers snap crackling away;
And clots the blood in a pulseless mass,
On the rim of the circle that none may pass.

'Or far and away in the Indian sea,
On the warm tropic nights, when the countless lights
  Of ocean flashed incessantly,
We would climb to the brow of some coral isle,
Some wonderful, glittering, ivory pile,
Plumed with proud young cocoa-nut trees,
Swinging and laughing in every breeze,

As if it were something one's leaves to toss
Under the light of the Southern Cross!
And there would we sit in our blithe retreat,
Till skies were glazed with morning heat,
And angrily scattering sparks and flame,
Out of the ocean the broad sun came.

' Or would we watch the strong ships dashing
 High overhead through the wind-white foam ;
The mad waves over their broad bows flashing,
 Steadily bound for a distant home.

' Some bore fruits of a wealthy region,
 Sheaves of silk, and clots of ore ;
Some were of War's wild sea-legion,
 Eager to smite upon wave or shore.

' Fleets beneath whose graceful wings
 Slept the fire that shakes the world ;
That "last argument of kings,"
 Through all time so rashly hurled.

' We saw that huge Armada sweep,
 Three hundred years ago,
Whose shadow darkened half the deep,
 And 'woe to England—woe ! '
Its priestly watchword heard we blown
From rear to van in a priestly tone,
" For God hath made our cause his own ! "

' Down came the ships of England,
 Their decks were dumb as death,

No cry was there, but a sailor's prayer
  In every deep-drawn breath :
No shout until stout Effingham
  Cried, " Britons, win the day !
God and the Queen ! " and then, I ween,
  A hundred miles away
The ringing cheer a man might hear,
  That told the fight begun,
As writhing broke white floors of smoke
  From every opening gun—
As at each blast a Spanish mast
  Went reeling by the board,
And momently more fierce and fast,
  The driving shot-storm roared !

' " Fight, Spaniards ! fight, Lepanto-men !
  Remember Corinth-bay !
Fight, stormers of the sea-wolf den !
  God fight for Spain to-day ! "

' No ! vain the shout. That fleet of pride
Shall ne'er again in roadstead ride,
  Nor lord it on the deep.
With sails shot loose and standards struck,
Crushed in one wild tumultuous ruck,
  They press like hunted sheep ;
Till yelling from our darkest caves,
Rushed all the ruin of the waves,
At His high voice who reared of old
This Isle of England—Freedom's hold,
And bade her sons be strong in fight,
And firm in faith, and wise in might,

To win their walls of roaring foam
A prouder name—the Exile's home.

'Enough—and more! O, trust them not,
   Who teach that Pleasure's blithest round
Can ever clear one conscience-blot,
   Or dull one still accusing sound;
Or charm the weary curse away,
   The blight upon our pathway-ground,
The rainless cloud that hides the day,
   From which our very prayers rebound.
The shadow that so slowly grew,
   We recked not of its broadening span;
Who ever in the morning knew
   How first some ominous dream began?

'By night there stood my couch beside
   A shrouded form with golden hair;
By day I watched it softly glide,
   A shade upon the windless air.
The step—the form, too well I knew,
And, oh! dishonoured and untrue,
I vainly strove with curse and frown
To beat the mournful phantom down:
To drain the wine-can with a laugh,
And say—"She was too soft by half!
Others have borne such jilt, and she
Need surely ne'er have died for me."

'Ah, blinded fool! what man may bide
Between the moon and rising tide,
And thunder to the marching sea
Words that may make him turn and flee?

Yet sooner should those headlong waves
Reel humbly back, like beaten slaves,
Than stern Remorse her task unlearn,—
The slow, sure foot of Vengeance turn!
It came at last! In mercy spare
The sight—the horror—the despair!
Enough, that it was Violet!
Enough?—ah, no! till I forget
The flutter of that coarse black pall,
The look—the tones—that told me all!

'That night—it was a custom old
  That all the viceroys of the Sea
Should, once a year, high banquet hold,
  And join in Ocean revelry—
That night our palace windows flung
A fourfold blaze the waves among;
Within, the tables cracked with gold,
The torches waved—the music rolled,
Aladdin's tower or Sindbad's dale,
Heaped ankle-deep with diamond hail,
Were dim to that vast vaulted hall,
Lit for a grand sea-festival.

'In royal beauty flushed with pride,
Beside me sat my queenly bride.
Too well she knew some secret pain
Racked my crushed heart—and long in vain
Had worked with Love's own tenderness,
To make the weary burden less.
Ah! double bitterness! I knew
She thought I pined for Earth's green hue,

For friends long left ; herself no more
The prized—the beautiful of yore.
There is not in the arrow-sheaf
Of black Remorse, a sharper grief
Than that which stings us when we know
Some loving bosom bleeds with woe,
Caught from our own—accusing still
Itself half author of the ill,
While we to soothe at least *its* pain,
Strive with our sin-locked lips in vain.

' And when the halls were cleared for wine,
   And the loud horn-peals blithely rang,
I felt a timid hand on mine,
   Alas, its very touch a pang !
As if unconscious of my woe,
   Although her own sweet eyes were wet,
She spoke, she smiled—as hoping so
   To cheat me of some fond regret.
Ah, trusting, lovely Oriande !
   Such memories as these with me,
Strike sharper than the fury-band
   That pay my broken oath to thee !
And then when jovial glees were roared
From mouth to mouth around the board,
As if before a flowing lay
Trouble and care must melt away,
   She beckoned to her side
That ancient harper of the Sea,
   And bade him sound, with all his pride,
A song that all of Love should be !

' Strange were the chords that, sharp and bold,
Clashed from the shivering strings of gold,

And sudden silence fell
On all the tables of the feast—
Laughter and jest and music ceased
    As at some wizard spell.
Like the dead lull it seemed when stirs
No spire of all the mountain firs
    Beneath a gathering sky,
The calm that in a moment more
Rings to the storm's advancing roar,
    As the first lightnings fly.
And shuddering in my guilt, I knew
That every eye the wide hall through
    At once was turned on me,
And in the dying of those chords,
Flashed through me like a thousand swords,—
    " Of Love my song shall be ! "
The prophet-harper sternly said,
" A funeral dirge for Love the dead,
    Sung under the salt sea."

    *   *   *   *   *

' 'Tis told ! I heard, yet heard it not—
The strain harp-thundered sharp and hot,
The bloodhound bay that tracked me down,
From Earth and knighthood's lost renown,
To double perjury, and there
Laid my last hideous treason bare !

' Then with confusion's clamour shook
    The startled halls. I saw no more—
Hiding my eyes lest they should look
    On her whose bright, brief dream was o'er.

Who dragged me forth her throne before
I know not—shuddering at a sound
Of thunder thrilled the marble floor,
And rang the purple panes around.

' Pale, bloodless, like a marble form,
She stood—around her hushed the storm,
Till from her lips each syllable
Upon these ears a fire-drop fell.

' "Not mine the doom," she slowly said,
"That lights upon thy shameless head.
Not mine the laws that warn thee hence
Beyond our Ocean's outmost fence,
To purge, in penitence and pain,
Thy bosom of this burning stain.
The stern old statutes of the sea
Leave, here, no two-way path for me.
Go forth, and, sworn upon the sun
To look no more, in blindness go:
Think upon those thou hast undone,
And share their bitter draught of woe.
Go forth! To speak of pardon here
Were idle, but while hope remains,
Let penance work thy spirit clear,
And lonely vigils cleanse thy veins.
It may be there are days in store
That still may link with days of yore;
It may be—ah, to Heaven atone,
Nor plead there for thyself alone!"

' Poor child! she could no more repress
Her bursting heart's great bitterness.
The queen-like mien, the tones were gone,

Weeping she sank my breast upon;
"O, more than half the fault was mine!"
She said—"yet what a doom is thine!
Forgive me—no! then hate me not,
Who share in heart at least thy lot;
The deepest draught in Sorrow's well
Henceforth is mine as thine—farewell!"

'So broke the morning of my dream;
   I heard the brazen gates clash fast;
I stood beside the fairy-stream
   And knew that all but pain was past.

'Since then what waste of years hath run
   I ill can tell—they pass me by
With barren change of frost and sun;
   Years are for those that live and die.

'I hoped at first: I hope no more.
   Yet, raft-rocked on a burning sea,
The death-struck sailor dreams of shore,
   And so it often is with me.

'Would it were else! that grace were mine
   These rusting links at once to sever;
To bid my soul no longer pine,
   When the Gates of the Ocean are fast for ever!'

Meanwhile the climbing moon had gained
   Her place on Heaven's deserted throne,
And the deep river, silver-veined,
   Like molten lava moved and shone.

A death-like silence held the trees;
   A charm came o'er the glittering night:
Believe or doubt me—which you please,
   I heard the cold stars blinking bright.

But, hark! a round of magic bells,
   A chaunt amid the willows ringing,
A long triumphant blast of shells,
   A swarm of lamps blue sparkles flinging!
The river has turned in his haunted bed,
And backward winds to his fountain head,
The fluttering leaves on each trembling tree
Have caught the breath of the distant sea,
The cliffs are echoing stone by stone,
The call of the bugle so clearly blown.

The first light notes had scarcely died,
Ere burst the old man from my side;
'Huzza, the bugles of the Sea!
There!—there again! they sound for Me!
Now, Heaven be thanked!'
                        No more he said,
But headlong in the river-bed
Plunged as he spoke: a joyous cry
Shook shore and water, trees and sky!
I saw the flashing lamps descend,
I heard a roar of *Bring your friend!*
And with a shocking start I woke,
Capsized across the fallen oak!

THE END.

www.ingramcontent.com/pod-product-compliance
Lightning Source LLC
Chambersburg PA
CBHW021402230426
43666CB00006B/608